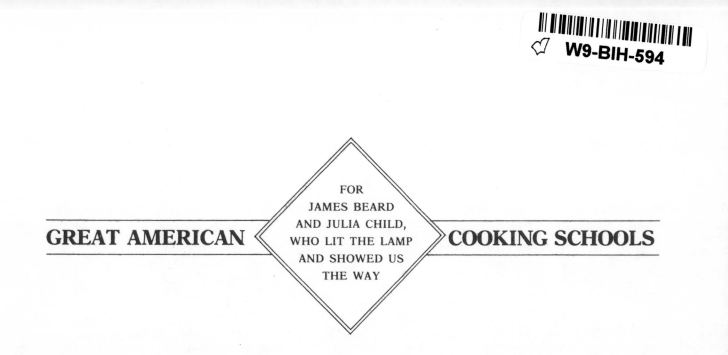

GREAT AMERICAN

FOR
JAMES BEARD
AND JULIA CHILD,
WHO LIT THE LAMP
AND SHOWED US
THE WAY

COOKING SCHOOLS

GREAT AMERICAN COOKING SCHOOLS

American Food & California Wine
Bountiful Bread: Basics to Brioches
Christmas Feasts from History
Romantic & Classic Cakes
Cooking of the South
Dim Sum & Chinese One-Dish Meals
Fine Fresh Food—Fast
Fresh Garden Vegetables
Ice Cream & Ices
Omelettes & Soufflés
Pasta! Cooking It, Loving It
Quiche & Pâté
Soups & Salads
Successful Parties: Simple & Elegant

Fine Fresh Food Fast

MICHELE URVATER

ILLUSTRATED BY ISADORE SELTZER

IRENA CHALMERS COOKBOOKS, INC. • **NEW YORK**

IRENA CHALMERS COOKBOOKS, INC.

PUBLISHER
Irena Chalmers

Sales and Marketing Director
Diane J. Kidd

Managing Editor
Jean Atcheson

Series Design
Helene Berinsky

Cover Design
Milton Glaser
Karen Skelton, *Associate Designer*

Cover Photography
Matthew Klein

Editor for this book
Richard Atcheson

Typesetting
J&J Graphics, Greensboro, NC

Printing
Lucas Litho, Inc., Baltimore

Editorial Offices
23 East 92nd Street
New York, NY 10028
(212) 289-3105

Sales Offices
P.O. Box 322
Brown Summit, NC 27214
(919) 656-3115

ISBN # 0-941034-02-X
© 1981 by Michele Urvater. All rights reserved.
Printed and published in the United States of America
by Irena Chalmers Cookbooks, Inc.
**LIBRARY OF CONGRESS
CATALOG CARD NO.: 81-68836**
  Urvater, Michele
    Fine fresh food-fast.

  Greensboro, NC: Chalmers, Irena Cookbooks
  84 p.
  8108   810722
    B C D E 5 4 3 2
      6 9 5 3

Contents

Acknowledgments

I am grateful to Irena Chalmers for putting this series together, and for giving a chance to so many of the cooking teachers of this country.

Enormous thanks go to my husband, Michael Cook, who continues, throughout the years and the recipes, to show unbounded enthusiasm for my work.

And, of course, the biggest thanks of all go to my students and friends—Bill Ayers, Nancy Davis, Candy Early, Connie Gardner, Barbara Gorin, Ann Linden, Susan Merians, Peter Rothschild, Bobby Rothstein, Sone Takahara and Susan Ginsberg Webman—whose testing of all the recipes insures that they work for everyone.

About the Author

Knowing how to eat well is important for every cook. Fortunately, I learned to eat in Belgium, one of Europe's great gastronomic countries, where the cooking easily rivals that of France and Italy.

Because both my parents were Belgian and loved good eating, I grew up with it from childhood. But my culinary education really began in my seventh year, when my family moved to Antwerp. There I was exposed to the characteristic ingredients of that region, such as succulent white asparagus, giant sugary strawberries, tiny sweet shrimp and dark bittersweet chocolate. Significantly, I also was blessed with an eccentric uncle, who was widely known in Europe as much for his demanding palate as for his celebrated art collection. Only the most subtle and freshest food, the greatest wines and the most perfect restaurants interested him. And even at that level, he often left unsatisfied. Many a time I sat with him at the table, cringing with embarrassment when he returned bottles of wine to the cellar, or dishes to the kitchen. But I did learn about perfection. When he was pleased, the meal had indeed been superb.

With my appetite developed in this way, it is no wonder that, when I came to live in the United States, I continued to seek out what I had become accustomed to. Eventually that led to the meshing of my career with my gourmandise.

My meager budget, when I was a student in America, did not permit me to indulge my taste for expensive restaurants. Instead, I decided to duplicate some of my gastronomic memories in my own kitchen. Thus my serious culinary training began.

At first, Julia Child's first book was my bible and I thought she was my master. But I soon realized that I had acquired countless culinary techniques on my own, from having observed our housekeeper-cooks during my youth. They had always discharged their culinary obligations to the family with all the artistry of accomplished chefs.

For a time, I practiced my art only on friends and relatives, but my passion pushed me farther. After taking every worthwhile private cooking course I could find in the New York area, I jumped into chef-dom by attending the New York City College Hotel School.

This professional education taught me how to transform the art of cooking dinner for six into the moneymaking skill of preparing meals for hundreds. Without this training, I never could have performed as I did, for one year, as chef in a Manhattan neighborhood restaurant. I cooked a different menu three nights of the week, for up to as many as 120 people. But I tired of devoting weekends, holidays—almost every living moment—to the restaurant, so I switched to day work, and became the chef for a small executive dining room at a financial magazine.

During this time friends, and friends of friends, begged me to teach them how to cook. After months of resisting, I gave in and set up a small class. To my astonishment I found that I loved teaching nearly as much as cooking. That is how my cooking school started seven years ago.

My classes have always emphasized taste. I want my students to taste, and eat, and eat, and taste. I want them to understand the importance of ingredients, to see how flavors change, develop, mature and finally come together into rounded whole tastes. In order to learn to love food, ingredients and taste, students have to be closely involved with each task, so I limit my classes to six students and all are expected to participate.

I divide my classes into three courses. The first is an eight-week course in comprehensive skills that teaches the principles underlying all cooking. I group recipes according to technique. The course progresses from stocks and soups to fish, meat, poultry, eggs, vegetables, sauces and desserts.

The second course, taught in six weeks, emphasizes more complex techniques, such as boning a whole chicken or a fish, and stresses the more difficult baking skills, such as croissant- and brioche-making.

Finally, for those students who wish to continue, I teach a menu course that includes French classic and nouvelle cuisine dishes.

Usually, after all of that, my students care about food and cooking nearly as much as I do.

Introduction

My cooking classes focus on classic French techniques which, as we all know, can be complex and time-consuming. However, many of my recipes can be cooked quickly, and much of what I teach is easy. In fact, it gives me great pleasure to help busy people continue to cook well, however short of time they may be, by compiling recipes which can be prepared and cooked in an hour.

Freshness in food is what I always stress, whether in quick or elaborate recipes. The quality of the ingredients is crucial to the excellence of a dish. And, although it is difficult in certain parts of the country to find fresh ingredients, freshness is important enough to encourage. I insist on it, not out of snobbery but because I am convinced that demand eventually influences supply. We have only to look at how the availability of ingredients has improved everywhere in the last 15 years to know that we all must continue to demand fresh, high-quality ingredients in order to ensure their continued accessibility.

The word "fresh" implies quality, but it is not enough to procure fresh ingredients if they are not good. The hard green tomatoes we buy in winter are "fresh," but they are so tasteless that they are infinitely inferior to canned varieties.

All the recipes in this book were selected because they can be prepared and cooked within an hour, so it is doubly important to select your ingredients carefully. For example, you must choose a cut of meat that will not require long marination or patient simmering. When you cook quickly, the inherent flavor, texture and quality of ingredients are immediately apparent.

To avoid the trap that often accompanies quick cooking—the less time you spend on a recipe, the more it has to cost—I use some ingredients that are inexpensive, but atypical of classic French cuisine. Bulgur wheat, a staple in Middle Eastern cooking, has a texture and flavor that rival rice, but never appears on French menus. Bean curd, a soybean product familiar to students of Oriental cooking, is not used in the Western kitchen, but it has such marvelous properties adaptable to quick cooking that I used it freely in several recipes. This is why, every now and then, you will see the use of ingredients not usually associated with the cuisine I teach.

Recipes that are quick to prepare often rely on simple techniques. Only twice do I suggest very delicate techniques—for a sauce thickened with butter, and for a dessert sauce thickened with egg yolks. Otherwise, the most complicated techniques I use here are the beating and folding of egg whites and the making of an egg-and-butter emulsion in a béarnaise. I included such techniques deliberately in order to associate them with simple recipes and to dispell the misconception that only experienced cooks can manage them.

To assemble this collection of recipes, I drew first, from the repertoire of my classes, those recipes that lend themselves most appropriately to the title; second, I developed some recipes that are entirely original with this book. All of them are illustrative of the techniques I regularly teach in class—techniques that are designed to make your kitchen preparation not only fresh and fast, but as fine as it can possibly be.

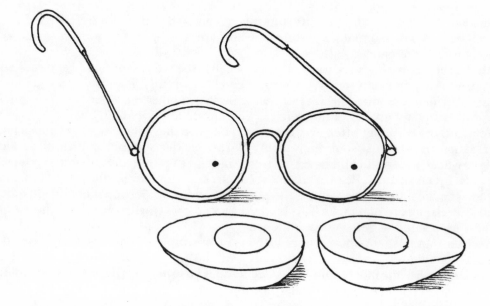

Ingredients

ARUGULA: A slightly peppery green, most often used in Italian cooking. Remove most of the stem before using and wash the leaves carefully, as the plant is very gritty. Arugula leaves are a wonderful addition to salads.

BACON: If possible, buy nitrite-free bacon and store all leftovers in the freezer.

BEAN CURD (TOFU): A wonderful, highly nutritious by-product of cooked soybeans. It is sold in square cakes, stored in water. It is unobtrusive enough to be versatile and blend with whatever you are cooking. Available in Chinese or Japanese food stores; store it always covered, in water, in the refrigerator.

BULGUR WHEAT: Wheat that is cooked, parched and then broken into pieces. This is *the* grain of Middle Eastern cuisine and makes a wonderful substitute for rice.

BUTTER: I always use unsalted butter because it has a fresher and sweeter flavor.

CHICKEN STOCK: When a recipe calls for chicken stock, it is really preferable to make your own. (Recipes for making stock abound in the culinary literature so I did not include one in this volume.) If you do buy canned stock, be sure to remove the surface fat before using it.

CHOCOLATE: When buying chocolate to cook with, look for a quality eating chocolate. An indication of quality chocolate is the amount of cocoa in it. Anything from 50 per cent upward is good. Semi-sweet chocolate is another term for bittersweet chocolate, which should not be confused with bitter or unsweetened chocolate, which has no sugar in it at all.

CIDER, HARD: A slightly alcoholic apple beverage available in liquor stores.

COARSE SALT: Also known as kosher salt. This is a coarse-grained salt, which has no anti-caking agents or iodine added. It dissolves more slowly than regular salt, so keep this in mind when seasoning a dish just before serving it.

CREAM: If possible buy "heavy" or "whipping" cream, which has not been ultra-pasteurized.

EGGS: All recipes in this book were tested with U.S. Grade A large eggs.

FLOUR: All recipes in this book were tested with all-purpose unbleached flour.

MUSTARD, DRY: This refers to the powdered dry mustard available in supermarkets.

MUSTARD, PREPARED: This is the regular mustard available in jars. The recipes in this book call for a strong French Dijon mustard.

OILS: I use different oils depending on the flavor I want. Olive oil, which I like and refer to in my recipes, is a pungent, extra-virgin oil that comes from the first pressing of the olives. I particularly like the French and Italian imported varieties, but you will have to experiment with different types to determine which ones you most prefer.

Walnut oil should be an imported French kind that has a strong, real nut flavor. The type available in our health food stores is just not tasty enough. After they are open, store all oils in a cool dark place or, short of that, in the refrigerator.

PARMESAN: The best kind to buy is the authentic, very expensive imported cheese from Italy. This is known as Parmigiano-Reggiano.

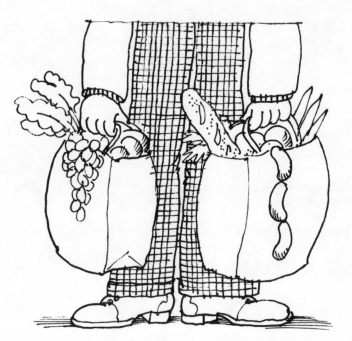

PARSLEY: I recommend the flat-leaf Italian parsley for flavor, but the curly type will do when you mince it for garnish.

PEPPERCORNS: Reserve white peppercorns for pale-hued dishes. Keep white and black peppercorns in separate grinders to avoid any risk of confusing them. It is essential to use only pepper that has been freshly ground each time from whole peppercorns.

SHALLOTS: These are part of the onion family. They have a distinctive flavor, not duplicated by any other member of the onion family. But if they are hard to find, you can use either onions or scallions.

SUGAR, SUPERFINE: A finely granulated sugar that dissolves "instantly" and is thus also known as "instant" sugar. This type of sugar is recommended in recipes which require no cooking to dissolve the sugar. You can make an approximate version at home by pulverizing granulated sugar in a food processor.

TOMATOES, CANNED: Fresh sweet tomatoes are always preferable to canned. But when fresh tomatoes are not in season, then it is perfectly acceptable to use a good brand of canned tomatoes. The best variety are the plum tomatoes from the San Marzano region of Italy.

TOMATO SAUCE: If you do not have a homemade tomato sauce on hand, use a commercial one containing only tomatoes, onions, garlic and seasoning. Stay away from brands that are heavy in sugar and additives. You can always improve on a canned variety by simmering the sauce with additional vegetables and seasonings of your choice.

VINEGARS: The best wine vinegars come from the Orléans region of France. Balsamic vinegar is an incredibly smooth, mild, sweet vinegar from the Modena region of Italy. It is so soft that it can be used in a higher proportion to oil than can most other vinegars. Rice vinegar is a sweet vinegar available in Oriental food stores. It too has a rather soft flavor.

Techniques and Terms

BEURRE BLANC: This refers to a sauce which is simply a highly acidic reduction of white wine vinegar and shallots into which is beaten a great deal of butter. When properly executed, a beurre blanc should be a satiny warm emulsion. You will achieve the correct consistency, without the sauce separating, if you take care to whisk in very cold butter over very low heat.

BOIL: When a liquid moves around furiously, sending large bubbles of air up to the surface, it is at a boil. Very few foods actually benefit from boiling because violent cooking toughens protein. It is usually best for parboiling vegetables or for rapid evaporation of a liquid.

BREADCRUMBS: To make "fresh" breadcrumbs, pulverize fresh, crustless bread in a food processor. The crumbs will be large, moist and spongy. To make "dry" breadcrumbs, use either stale bread or toast the bread in the oven until dry. Then pulverize it in a food processor or blender.

CHOP: In culinary terms, this means to cut food into uneven pieces about half an inch in size.

CHOP FINELY: This is the term for cutting food into uneven pieces about a quarter of an inch in size.

DEGLAZE: After sautéeing or roasting, there can be pieces of coagulated juices that have leaked out of the food and have stuck to the pan. They are full of flavor and should not be discarded. To loosen them, add a liquid, such as stock, wine or water to the pan. Bring it to a boil while scraping these browned particles into the liquid. The particles dissolve in the liquid; this is known as "deglazing" the pan.

DEVEIN: Cut a notch down the curved back of a peeled shrimp, to expose the large green-and-black intestine, in order to remove it.

DICE: Cut food into even squares, which are usually an eighth or a quarter of an inch in size.

FOLD: This term usually refers to folding beaten egg whites into a dense base. To do so, first lighten the base by adding some egg whites to it. When you incorporate the egg whites into the base, do so with a rubber spatula which you cut into the dense base, folding egg whites into it as you work. Do not stir or you deflate the egg whites. Once you have lightened the base, fold in the remaining egg whites.

GRATE: Form thin strips or shreds by rubbing food over metal holes of a hand-held grater or by using the grating blade of a food processor.

GRATE LEMON RIND: Scrape the yellow outer skin of a lemon by rubbing it on small holes of a grater. Do not rub white pith on grater or the rind will be bitter.

JULIENNE: Cut food into matchstick-sized or slightly larger pieces.

MINCE: Chop food into such fine pieces that it is close to pureed.

NUTS: To *roast* nuts, place them on a baking sheet and bake in a preheated 375-degree oven for 15 to 20 minutes, or until they emit a toasted aroma and turn golden brown. To *grind* nuts properly without extracting their oils, pulverize them in a food processor or grate them with a hand-held rotary grater.

PARBOIL: This means to cook food briefly in boiling water until it is partially cooked.

POACH: This is the process of cooking food gently while it is submerged in a liquid that is barely moving. Bubbles should only occasionally break the surface of the liquid. The process is used to cook fragile foods so that they do not fall apart, or for slow dishes such as braises or stews.

REDUCE: The term means to evaporate a liquid rapidly by boiling, in order to concentrate its flavor and reduce its volume.

Sauté: The process of cooking food in a small quantity of fat, over medium to high heat, in order to seal in the juices, brown the outside and form a crust. To sauté food successfully, be sure the fat is hot before you add food to the skillet. Be sure also that you do not crowd the pan, or the food will turn soggy.

Sear: Cook something briefly on every side, over fairly high heat, in order to seal in the juices.

Season: Add salt and pepper to taste.

Seed: Spoon out unwanted seeds, as in cucumbers or tomatoes, so that the vegetable does not exude too much water.

Simmer: The term is closely related to poaching, but implies cooking at a slightly higher heat. It, too, refers to cooking food submerged in a liquid that is barely moving. The term is used most frequently in relation to slow-cooking dishes.

Steam: To cook food by the steam that rises above a boiling liquid. The food must be raised above and out of the boiling liquid. To do so, use a metal steamer which has three legs that sit in the pot and keep it out of the liquid.

Whisk: To whisk is to stir with a wire whip. This technique should be used when trying to blend a compact mass into a fluid one, as when whisking butter into a sauce.

Equipment

DOUBLE BOILER (BAIN MARIE): A combination of equipment consisting of one vessel for food that fits inside a slightly larger vessel holding boiling water. The heat of the boiling water cooks the food. This is used for delicate foods, which would suffer from the heat of direct cooking or from high temperatures. A double boiler can be purchased for the purpose, or one can easily be approximated at home by fitting a small pot into a larger one.

FOOD MILL: A hand-operated metal or plastic pureeing device that comes with three discs. One is for grating; the other two, of varying degrees of fineness, are reserved for pureeing.

GRATER, HAND-HELD: A four-sided metal grater that stands on a counter or flat surface. One side is used to slice; the other three sides are used for grating to varying degrees of fineness.

GRATER, ROTARY: A metal or plastic hand-held grater that comes with rotary discs of varying degrees of fineness. This machine is perfect for grating cheese and chocolate, because it does not pulverize these to the degree that a food processor does.

STEAMER: A round, stainless steel device that sits on three legs and has folding adjustable flaps. The flaps permit the steamer to be used in pots of different sizes.

THERMOMETERS: When performing a culinary operation in which the outcome depends on exact temperatures—in deep-frying, for example, or in sugar work—always use a thermometer. Taylor manufactures a reliable brand of culinary thermometers.

Recipes

*In the following recipes, this signifies the point to which a dish can be prepared ahead of time.

APPETIZERS

Bean Curd Salad

Makes 4 servings

If bean curd (tofu) is hard to obtain, substitute two ounces of peeled and parboiled cold shrimp for each portion of bean curd. If you have the time, let the dressing stand for one hour so that the flavor of the garlic softens and permeates the sauce. This is a pungent appetizer, so follow it with an equally strong entree, such as Bluefish and Fennel.

4 tablespoons lemon juice
½ teaspoon grated lemon rind
Sliver of garlic, about
   1 inch by ½ inch
⅓ cup roasted cashews or peanuts
⅓ cup packed parsley leaves,
   washed
½ cup walnut or peanut oil
4 large leaves of Boston lettuce,
   washed
14 ounces fresh bean curd
2 tablespoons sweet red pepper,
   finely diced
Salt
Freshly ground pepper

In a blender or food processor, combine the lemon juice, lemon rind, garlic, nuts, parsley, oil, ¾ teaspoon salt and ¼ teaspoon pepper. Blend until smooth.

Center a Boston lettuce leaf on each of four salad plates. Dice bean curd into neat ½-inch squares and center a portion on each lettuce leaf. Spoon the dressing over the bean curd and sprinkle diced red pepper over the top.

Mushrooms Stuffed with Parsley-Garlic Butter   *Makes 6 servings*

Filled mushrooms are often heavy when stuffed with a mixture thickened with breadcrumbs. These particular mushrooms, however, are light because the filling is made only with fresh parsley, lemon juice, garlic, pine nuts and butter. Serve this as a starter before an entree of equally powerful taste, such as Lamb with Feta Cheese and Tomatoes.

3 ounces parsley, washed
24 mushroom caps, about 2½ inches
** in diameter**
6 tablespoons butter, at room
** temperature**
2 tablespoons pine nuts
2 cloves garlic
1 tablespoon lemon juice
Salt
Freshly ground pepper
3 slices wholewheat bread,
** about ½ inch thick**

Preheat the broiler.

Remove and discard as many of the parsley stems as possible.

Wipe each mushroom cap with a damp towel. Remove the stems and reserve them for some other use.

In a blender or food processor, combine 4 tablespoons of the butter with the parsley, pine nuts, garlic, lemon juice, ½ teaspoon salt and ¼ teaspoon pepper. Process until finely pureed. Stuff some of this mixture into each mushroom cap and place the caps on a baking sheet.

Halve each slice of bread, so that you have 6 triangles.

Sauté the bread triangles in the remaining butter until they are golden-brown on both sides. Salt them lightly and set aside.*

Just before serving, broil the mushrooms about 2 inches away from the heat, for about 5 minutes, or until they begin to soften and the butter is almost completely melted. Serve the mushrooms on the toast.

Sautéed Mozzarella with Fresh Tomatoes

Makes 4 servings

Unexpected contrasts lie in the juxtaposition of the slightly salty hot cheese with the sweet, cold tomato wedges. Be sure to use rich-tasting tomatoes so that the subtle combination of flavors will be fully realized. Multiply or divide this recipe according to how many people you intend to serve.

½ pound mozzarella cheese
¾ cup fresh breadcrumbs
¼ cup Parmesan cheese, grated
2 teaspoons oregano
1 egg beaten with 2 teaspoons olive oil
2 very ripe tomatoes, at room temperature
2 tablespoons olive oil
2 tablespoons butter
1 tablespoon parsley, minced
Salt
Freshly ground pepper

Cut the mozzarella cheese into 8 pieces, each ½ inch thick and about 2½ by 1½ inches wide. Combine the breadcrumbs with the Parmesan, ½ teaspoon salt, ¼ teaspoon pepper and oregano. Dip pieces of mozzarella into the egg-and-oil mixture, then pat the crumb mixture around each piece. Let them set on a plate, in the refrigerator, for 10 minutes.*

Just before serving, cut each tomato into 8 wedges. Have 4 salad plates ready.

Heat the olive oil and butter in a 9-inch skillet until hot. Sauté the mozzarella pieces, over medium heat, for about 1½ minutes per side. With a spatula transfer 2 pieces of cheese to the center of each plate; place a tomato wedge on either side. Dust the tomatoes with the parsley, and serve.

Carrot, Celery and Egg Salad

Makes 4 servings

Though the ingredients are plain, this salad has a remarkably good taste. Be sure to squeeze out all the moisture from the celery or you will dilute the dressing. Serve this as a first course, or as a side dish.

½ pound carrots, peeled
¾ pound celery
2 hard-boiled eggs
½ cup mayonnaise
3 tablespoons lemon juice
Salt
Freshly ground pepper
Optional: Boston lettuce leaves or spinach leaves, washed

Grate the carrots on the large holes of a hand grater or in a food processor. Set them in a bowl. Grate the celery and, with your hands, squeeze out as much moisture as possible. Add the celery to the carrots.

Dice the eggs into small pieces and add to the carrots and celery. Blend the lemon juice into the mayonnaise and add to the salad. Season with salt and pepper and mix all the ingredients well together. Refrigerate until ready to use.*

You may serve this on Boston lettuce or spinach leaves.

Ricotta Cheese Soufflés

These are almost absurdly easy to make, but remarkably impressive to guests. Be sure to bake them in a bain marie, to keep them moist and tender. Do not expect an enormous lift—the soufflés just rise gently.

1 tablespoon butter, to grease molds
⅓ cup ricotta cheese
1 teaspoon prepared mustard
1 teaspoon oregano
Pinch cayenne pepper
3 ounces Parmesan cheese, grated
3 tablespoons milk
3 eggs, separated
Salt, to taste

Preheat oven to 400 degrees.

Generously butter 6 ramekins or custard dishes, each one about ½-cup capacity. Set aside.

Mix together the ricotta cheese, mustard, oregano, cayenne, Parmesan, milk and 3 egg yolks in a bowl until well blended.

In a clean bowl, with clean beaters, whip the egg whites with a pinch of salt until stiff. (Do not overdo this step or your soufflé will be dry.) Fold the egg whites into the cheese batter. Work fast so that you do not deflate the egg whites. Spoon some of the batter into each ramekin. Place them in a baking pan filled with enough hot water to come three-quarters of the way up the sides of the ramekins. Bake for 15 minutes. Serve the soufflés from the molds; their centers should be soft.

Souffléed Parsnip Pudding

The techniques employed here are similar to those used when making soufflés, but the texture is too dense for the dish to merit such a high-flown title. You must first cook the curry powder to remove its rather harsh raw taste. Although the curry is not clearly recognizable, it contributes a definite, flavor to the parsnips. The center of the pudding is runny and forms the perfect sauce for the firmer, outside parts.

5 tablespoons butter
1 pound parsnips, peeled and finely chopped
⅓ cup onion, finely chopped
¼ teaspoon curry powder
¾ cup heavy cream
1 teaspoon flour
3 egg yolks
Salt
Freshly ground white pepper
4 egg whites

Preheat oven to 400 degrees.

With 1 tablespoon of the butter, grease the inside of a 4-cup soufflé dish.

Heat the remaining butter in a 9-inch skillet. When hot, add the parsnips, onion and curry powder. Sauté for about 1 minute over medium heat. Cover the pan, lower the heat, and simmer for 15 to 20 minutes or until the onions and parsnips are soft. Transfer the mixture to a food mill or food processor and puree until smooth.

Whisk the heavy cream, flour, yolks, ¾ teaspoon salt and ¼ teaspoon pepper into the puree.*

Whip the egg whites with a pinch of salt until stiff but not dry. Fold the beaten egg whites into the parsnip puree, taking care to work fast so that you do not deflate the egg whites. Spoon this into the prepared soufflé dish and bake for 25 minutes.

NOTE: When peeling parsnips, cut them in half. If you see a wide whitish core, remove it; if the core is thin, leave it in.

Leek and Bacon Gratiné

Makes 6-8 servings

Basically a gratiné is a quiche without the crust. This recipe is less dense than ordinary gratinés because it has less cream and fewer eggs. You could serve it as an appetizer or as a lunch or supper dish, if you give copious servings and garnish each plate with a tossed green salad.

2 tablespoons butter
4 slices bacon
8 medium-size leeks
½ cup water
3 eggs
1 cup heavy cream
¼ teaspoon ground nutmeg
½ cup sharp cheddar cheese,
   grated
Salt
Freshly ground pepper

Preheat oven to 375 degrees.

With 1 tablespoon of butter, lightly grease an 8-inch pie plate.

Brown the bacon in a 10-inch skillet. While the bacon is browning, wash and slice the leeks into ½-inch rounds. When the bacon is brown, remove most of the bacon fat, then add the leeks and water to the skillet. Cover and simmer, over low heat, for 20 minutes, or until the leeks are tender and have absorbed the water. Evaporate any remaining water over medium heat, uncovered. Be sure to stir the leeks every now and then as they cook, to be sure they do not burn.

Remove the leeks and bacon to the bowl of a food processor or blender. Add the eggs, cream, nutmeg, ½ teaspoon salt and ¼ teaspoon pepper. Process or blend for a few seconds until the bacon is chopped up. (Do not overdo this step or you will end up with baby food.)

Pour this mixture into the prepared pie plate. Sprinkle grated cheese and pieces of the remaining tablespoon of butter on top. Bake for 25 minutes, or until the custard has set. Serve warm or tepid.

NOTE: You can reheat this in a 325-degree oven for 15 minutes.

SOUPS

Avocado and Tomato Soup

Makes 4 servings

This soup is not only super on a hot summer's night, but not half bad at any time of year! If you have the time, it is at its best when chilled overnight.

1 cup avocado, diced
3 tablespoons white onion, finely chopped
1 cup water
2 cups tomato juice
Grated rind of 1 lime
Juice of 1 lime
¼ cup sour cream
¼ cup mayonnaise
1 cucumber, peeled, seeded and diced
½ cup avocado, cut into ½-inch dice, for garnish
1 tablespoon parsley, minced
Salt
Freshly ground white pepper

Combine the first 8 ingredients in a food processor or blender and process until smooth. (You may have to do this in 2 batches so that your machine does not overflow.) Taste for seasoning and add salt and pepper.* Chill for 45 minutes or, preferably, overnight.

Garnish each portion with some diced cucumber, avocado and a sprinkling of parsley.

Cream of Turnip and Garlic Soup

Makes 4-6 servings

Turnips and garlic, ordinarily so pungent, lose their aggressive harshness when boiled, as they are here, for a long time. The resulting soup is delicate. The most distinctive flavor is, oddly enough, the Parmesan, which is added at the end.

1½ cups water
3 cups chicken stock, preferably homemade
½ pound white turnips, peeled and chopped
8 whole garlic cloves, peeled
1 bay leaf
¼ teaspoon dry thyme
2 egg yolks
½ cup heavy cream
½ cup Parmesan cheese, grated
Salt
Freshly ground white pepper
Paprika

Bring water, stock, turnips and garlic to a boil in a 2-quart, non-aluminum saucepan. Add the bay leaf, thyme, ½ teaspoon salt and ¼ teaspoon pepper. Cover, and simmer, on very low heat, for 30 minutes. Remove the bay leaf.

Puree the soup in a blender or food processor until smooth. Adjust the seasoning.*

Just before serving, whisk the egg yolks, heavy cream and cheese together in a bowl. Bring the soup back to a boil. Ladle some hot soup into the egg yolk mixture. Then add this mixture back to the simmering soup, whisking constantly. Whisk for 30 seconds, or until the soup thickens slightly. Do not let the soup boil or the eggs will scramble. Serve immediately, with a fine dusting of paprika.

NOTE: It is perfectly all right if the cheese does not melt completely.

American Oyster Soup

This is my favorite easy soup because it is as luxurious as it is simple to make. It consists of fresh oysters, briefly poached in cream and milk. If you buy the oysters already shucked, this recipe takes all of ten minutes to make.

2 dozen oysters, shucked; reserve oyster liquor
½ cup heavy cream
½ cup milk
½ teaspoon dry sherry
2 tablespoons butter
3 tablespoons parsley, minced
Salt
Freshly ground white pepper

Place oyster liquor and heavy cream in a 10-inch skillet. Reduce this over medium heat for about 1 minute. Add the oysters, milk, sherry, ½ teaspoon salt and a pinch of pepper. Heat over low heat until the edges of the oysters begin to curl. (Do not overdo this step or the oysters will toughen.) Turn the heat off and swirl the butter into the soup. Blend until it is completely incorporated into the soup; adjust the seasoning.

Ladle the soup into heated soup bowls and dust each one with parsley.

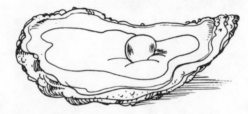

Rice, Carrot and Onion Soup

This soup is among my personal favorites because I never tire of its mellow, satisfying flavor. Believe it or not, the rice is what gives the soup its distinctive, dainty taste.

3 tablespoons butter
2 medium-size onions, finely chopped
3 medium-size carrots, finely chopped
1 quart chicken stock, preferably homemade
⅓ cup raw, long-grain white rice
½ cup heavy cream
1 tablespoon parsley, minced
Salt
Freshly ground pepper

Melt the butter in a 4-quart saucepan. When hot, stir in the onions and carrots. Cover, and simmer for 10 minutes, over low heat. Stir once to make sure the vegetables do not burn. Remove the cover, add the stock and rice, ¾ teaspoon salt and ¼ teaspoon pepper. Bring to a boil, and then simmer for 25 minutes more. Remove from the heat. Puree soup in a food mill, blender or food processor. Add the cream, bring the soup back to a simmer and adjust the seasoning.*

Transfer the soup to a tureen or heated soup plates and sprinkle with parsley before serving.

Spiced Peanut Soup

The best peanut butter is made from freshly ground peanuts. It is available in health food stores and in some supermarkets. If you cannot find non-homogenized peanut butter, then use the homogenized kind. The taste of this soup is complex and one is hard put to identify all the flavors—particularly the peanut butter.

2 tablespoons butter
2 slices bacon, finely diced
1 medium-size onion, thinly sliced
¼ pound sweet potatoes, peeled
¼ teaspoon each of ground
  cinnamon, chili powder, cumin
  and cayenne
3 cups chicken stock or water
2 tablespoons tomato paste
½ cup non-homogenized peanut
  butter
½ cup sour cream
Salt
Freshly ground pepper

Melt the butter over medium heat in a 3- or 4-quart saucepan; then add the bacon. After a couple of minutes, add the onion, then cover the pot and cook for about 10 minutes, or until the onion is translucent. Check the onion every now and then to make sure it is not burning.

While the onion is cooking, dice the potatoes. When the onion is translucent, remove the cover and stir in the potatoes, spices and stock. Cover, and simmer for 20 minutes.

Transfer the soup to a blender or food processor. Add the tomato paste and peanut butter and puree until smooth. Season with about ½ teaspoon salt and ¼ teaspoon pepper.*

Reheat the soup until piping hot; garnish each portion with a dab of sour cream.

NOTE: You may use boiling potatoes instead of sweet potatoes.

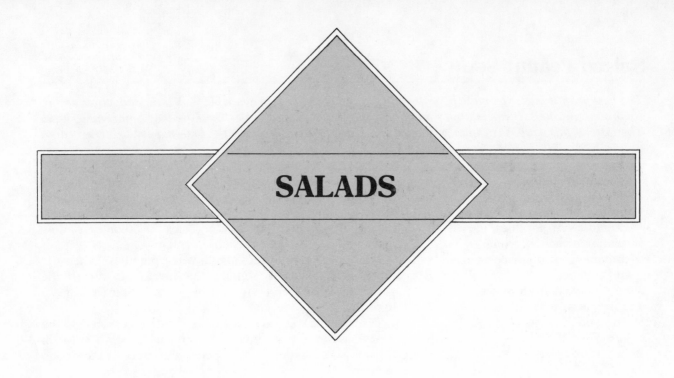

SALADS

Ham and Endive Remoulade

Makes 4 servings

When I was a little girl in Antwerp, we often ate a traditional Belgian dish: baked endives wrapped in ham. I have always liked the combination of flavors and have used it in this salad. The dressing is similar to one used in a celery remoulade.

½ **pound endives**
½ **pound baked ham, sliced into**
  ¼-inch slices
½ **cup mayonnaise**
2 **tablespoons lemon juice**
2 **tablespoons heavy cream**
1 **tablespoon prepared mustard**
¼ **teaspoon dry mustard**
½ **pound spinach, stemmed and**
  washed
Salt
Freshly ground pepper

Cut the root end off the endives. Separate the leaves and wipe off any sand with a damp cloth or a paper towel. Julienne them into approximately 2-inch-by-¼-inch pieces. Julienne the ham into similar pieces and set aside.

Combine mayonnaise, lemon juice, cream, and the prepared and dry mustards. Season to taste with salt and pepper. Add the dressing to endives and ham and toss. Taste for seasoning and adjust.

To serve, place a ring of spinach leaves on each plate and center a portion of salad in the middle. There is enough dressing in the endives and ham to moisten the spinach when you dig into the salad.

Green Salad

It might seem ridiculous to include something as simple as a green salad, but there are several steps in making a really superb salad which too many people omit. First, be sure the leaves are well washed and thoroughly dried. Do not make too much dressing or you will lose the flavor of the greens and they will wilt. For interest and variety, change the types of oils and vinegars. In this recipe, I use Balsamic vinegar, which is so mild and sweet that I use a larger proportion than I would with ordinary vinegars.

1 medium-size Boston lettuce
1 bunch arugula leaves
2 tablespoons walnut oil plus 2
  teaspoons
2 tablespoons Balsamic vinegar
Salt
Freshly ground pepper

Wash the lettuce in water and dry the leaves with a salad spinner or with towels until they are bone-dry. Then remove most of the arugula stems and discard any leaves that are brown or yellowish. Wash well in several changes of water, because arugula is extremely gritty. (But that nutty, peppery flavor makes it all worthwhile.) Dry the arugula leaves and add them to the Boston lettuce.

Mix 2 tablespoons of walnut oil with the vinegar. Set aside.

Just before serving, coat the salad greens with 2 teaspoons of oil. This makes the dressing adhere to the leaves. Then toss the salad with the dressing. Serve immediately.

NOTE: When washing greens in advance, keep them, refrigerated, loosely covered with a damp cloth. Do not pack them in an airtight plastic bag or the leaves will wilt and turn brown.

A more frequently used salad dressing consists of 1 part vinegar to 3 parts of oil.

Egg and Vegetable Salad

Makes 4 servings

Easily prepared, especially when hard-boiled eggs are on hand, this gorgeous salad, with its protein-laden eggs and vitamin-rich vegetables, makes a complete meal. Serve it in small quantities as an appetizer, or in heftier portions as a light summer supper.

1 head broccoli, cut in florets with only 2 inches of stem left on
8 hard-boiled eggs, peeled and quartered
1 large red pepper (about 2 cups julienned)
1 bunch watercress
½ cup mayonnaise
2 tablespoons prepared mustard
¼ cup lemon juice
Salt
Freshly ground pepper

Steam or boil the broccoli until cooked, but still crunchy. Refresh it under cold water and pat dry. Roughly dice it into 2-inch pieces. Combine this with the eggs and peppers.

Wash the watercress and cut off all but 1 inch of stem. Add the watercress to the eggs and other vegetables.

Combine the mayonnaise with mustard, lemon juice, salt and pepper. Toss this with all the ingredients. Taste for seasoning and adjust salt and pepper. Chill for 15 minutes.*

Shrimp and Grapefruit Salad

Makes 4 servings

The source of inspiration for this recipe was a dish composed of shrimp, oranges and anchovies. Because I found the oranges rather too sweet with shellfish, I substituted grapefruit, as I like the citrus flavor. It is refreshing and unusual and works well as an appetizer or as a lunch dish.

32 shrimp, medium or large
2 medium-size grapefruit
3 tablespoons walnut or peanut oil
3 tablespoons Champagne or rice vinegar
½ teaspoon prepared mustard
¼ cup red onion, finely chopped
Boston lettuce leaves, washed
Salt
Freshly ground white pepper

Peel and devein the shrimp. Bring 1 quart of water to a boil. Add shrimp and simmer them for about 1½ minutes. Remove the shrimp and refresh them under cold water. Cut the shrimp in half, along the indentation left by deveining them. Pat dry and place in a bowl.

With a sharp knife, remove all the skin and white pith around the grapefruits. Then cut into sections, *in between* the membranes, so that you entirely free each section from all the skin. Then cut each section in half so that you have approximately 1-inch pieces. Add these to the shrimp.

Beat the oil with the vinegar and mustard, along with ½ teaspoon salt and ¼ teaspoon pepper. Add this to the onion and pour over the shrimp and grapefruit. Toss together and taste for seasoning.

Serve directly, or chill for half an hour. Serve over Boston lettuce leaves.

Bulgur Wheat Salad with Cheese Dressing   *Makes 4-6 servings*

You can vary the vegetables that you add to this salad. For instance, substitute diced peeled carrots for the peppers, or finely diced raw zucchini for the cucumbers. However, if you decide to use a vegetable such as broccoli, which is high in cellulose, be sure to parboil it first.

1 cup bulgur wheat
¼ cup radishes, halved and thinly
   sliced
½ cup cucumbers, peeled, seeded
   and diced
½ cup sweet red peppers, finely
   diced
¼ cup celery, finely diced
¼ cup scallions, thinly sliced
¼ cup vegetable oil
3 tablespoons white wine vinegar
2 tablespoons plain yogurt
½ teaspoon prepared mustard
½ cup sharp cheddar cheese,
   grated
Lettuce leaves, washed
2 tomatoes, quartered or ½ cup
   cherry tomatoes
Salt
Freshly ground pepper

Bring 2 cups of water to a boil with ½ teaspoon salt. Pour this over the bulgur wheat and let the wheat stand for 20 minutes or until it is soft. Drain the wheat very well by placing it in a sieve, set over a bowl.

Add the radishes, cucumbers, peppers, celery and scallions to the well-drained wheat.

Make a dressing by beating together the oil, vinegar, yogurt, mustard and cheese. Season with ½ teaspoon salt and ¼ teaspoon pepper. Toss all the ingredients with the dressing and adjust the seasoning.*

Serve over lettuce leaves and garnish with tomatoes. Finish with a few generous grindings of fresh pepper over each serving.

PASTA

Tomato Fettucine with Broccoli and Roquefort
Makes 4 servings

The color combination of the pink pasta with the green broccoli is particularly appealing. If you have trouble finding a ripe and genuine Roquefort, substitute a good American blue cheese.

1 bunch broccoli, broken into florets
1¼ cups heavy cream
½ cup Roquefort cheese, crumbled
¾ pound tomato fettucine
½ cup Parmesan cheese, grated
Salt, to taste
Freshly ground pepper, to taste

Bring 2 quarts of water to a boil with 1 teaspoon salt. Boil the broccoli for 5 minutes, or until cooked but still crunchy. When the broccoli is cooked, drain it immediately and refresh it under cold water. When it is cool enough to handle, pat the florets dry and cut them into ½-inch pieces.* Heat the serving bowls.

To cook the pasta, bring 4 quarts of water to a boil with 1 tablespoon salt, in a large 6-quart pot. As the water comes to a boil, start the sauce.

Reduce the heavy cream in a 12-inch skillet over medium heat for about 1 minute. Add the cut-up broccoli and cook for 1 minute more. Add the Roquefort and keep the sauce simmering over low heat until the pasta is done. By then, the sauce should be sufficiently reduced. Taste the sauce for seasoning and add salt and a generous amount of freshly ground pepper.

When the pasta water comes to a boil, add the fettucine and cook for 4 minutes, or until just cooked but still slightly *al dente*. Drain and refresh under hot, not cold, water so that the pasta does not cool off.

To serve, place a portion of pasta in each heated bowl and ladle the sauce on top. Sprinkle Parmesan over the top, and allow each person to toss his own pasta.

Thin Spaghetti with Cold Herbed Butter   *Makes 4 servings*

I make this recipe with a pasta made from Jerusalem artichoke flour and it is simply wonderful. This type of pasta seems less starchy to me; it is readily available, under the brand name "DeBoles," in some supermarkets and in health food stores. It is well worth a try. If you cannot find it, substitute ordinary spaghetti.

¼ pound butter, softened
1½ tablespoons shallots, minced
2 tablespoons parsley, minced
1 tablespoon dried tarragon
1 tablespoon lemon juice
½ teaspoon grated lemon rind
½ cup cottage cheese
¾ pound thin spaghetti, made from
   Jerusalem artichoke flour
Salt
Freshly ground pepper

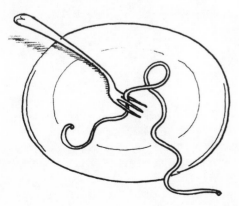

Beat all the ingredients, except for the pasta, in a bowl along with ½ teaspoon salt and ¼ teaspoon pepper. You can easily do this in a food processor.*

Heat up the serving bowl and plates.

Bring 4 quarts of water to a boil in a large pot with 1 tablespoon salt. When water is at a rolling boil, add the pasta and stir a couple of times, keeping the spaghetti circulating in the water. Let boil for 8 minutes. Drain, but do not refresh under cold water. Immediately, add the drained pasta to the heated serving bowl and add the butter-herb-and-cheese mixture. Toss until all the pasta strands are evenly coated with butter and herbs.

NOTE: It is important to heat both the serving bowl and dinner plates because the pasta tends to cool off rapidly. These portions are only appropriate for a first course or a side dish. As a main course, this would serve only 2 people.

Spinach Pasta with Mackerel and Tomato Sauce   *Makes 4 servings*

The sauce is so rich and full-bodied that this pasta recipe is more appropriate for a main course than for an appetizer or first course. It is important to remove the center, dark part of the filets to eliminate some of the strong fishy flavor. The taste of mackerel is potent; this is not a dish for weak palates. In fact, its flavor is hearty enough to demand a substantial red wine, such as a Cabernet Sauvignon.

¾ **pound mackerel filets**
¼ **cup olive oil**
1 teaspoon garlic, minced
4 canned anchovies, rinsed and finely chopped
⅓ **cup imported black olives, pitted and finely chopped**
2 tablespoons capers, rinsed and finely chopped
1½ **cups tomato sauce (can be a good canned variety)**
½ **cup Parmesan cheese, grated**
1 pound spinach fettucine
½ **teaspoon crushed red pepper**
Salt

In the center of each mackerel filet you will see a dark line with small bones protruding from it. Remove this and cut remaining fish into 2-inch chunks. Set aside.

To cook pasta, bring 4 quarts of water to a boil, with 1 tablespoon salt, in a large 6-quart pot. As the water is coming to a boil, proceed with the sauce. Heat serving plates.

Heat the olive oil in a 12-inch skillet. When hot, add garlic and sauté for about 30 seconds. Add anchovies, olives and capers and sauté for 1 minute. Add the tomato sauce and red pepper and stir until the sauce is bubbling. Add the fish chunks and stir over low heat for about 10 minutes, or until the fish looks flaky. Taste and season (you probably will not need any salt because of the anchovies and capers).

When the pasta water comes to a boil, add the fettucine and cook until cooked through but still *al dente*. Drain and refresh under hot water, not cold, so that you do not cool off the pasta.

To serve, place a portion of pasta in each heated plate, ladle some fish sauce over that and sprinkle on the Parmesan.

NOTE: If you cannot find spinach fettucine, substitute the ordinary kind.

Pasta with Goat Cheese, Ham and Dandelions

Makes 4-6 servings

When searching for goat cheese, look for cheese that is chalky white, without a runny, thick outer band of yellowish cheese. Do not buy wholewheat pasta in a health food store; it is a little too heavy. I prefer to use an imported brand made in Italy. If you cannot find it, then substitute regular fettucine. This is a rich and filling dish and should be served only as a main course.

1½ pounds dandelions, or other
    greens such as beet greens
½ pound smoky ham, thinly sliced
¾ pound goat cheese such as
    Montrachet or Bucheron
½ cup extra-virgin olive oil
2 garlic cloves, minced
2 teaspoons fresh rosemary, or
    ½ teaspoon dried and crumbled
½ cup heavy cream
1 pound wholewheat fettucine
Salt
Freshly ground pepper

Wash the dandelions, removing about 4 inches of stem, or up to the point the leaves start on the stalk. Discard the stalks. Chop the remaining dandelion leaves into approximately 2-inch pieces.

Julienne the ham into ½-inch pieces. Crumble the goat cheese.*

Bring 4 quarts of water to a boil with 2 teaspoons salt in a large pot. As the water is coming to the boil, start the sauce.

Heat the olive oil in a 12-inch skillet. Add the garlic. When the garlic is just beginning to turn golden, add the dandelions and sauté for about 1 minute, or until they start to wilt. Add the ham, goat cheese, rosemary and cream. Reduce until thick, and then season with salt and pepper. Keep warm over very low heat.

Meanwhile, boil the fettucine for about 6 minutes, or until cooked but still *al dente*. Or, follow the package directions. Drain the fettucine, but do not refresh under cold water.

To serve, place a portion of pasta in each person's plate, then ladle the sauce in the center, on top of the pasta. Let people do their own tossing at the dinner table to lessen the chances of the pasta cooling off too quickly.

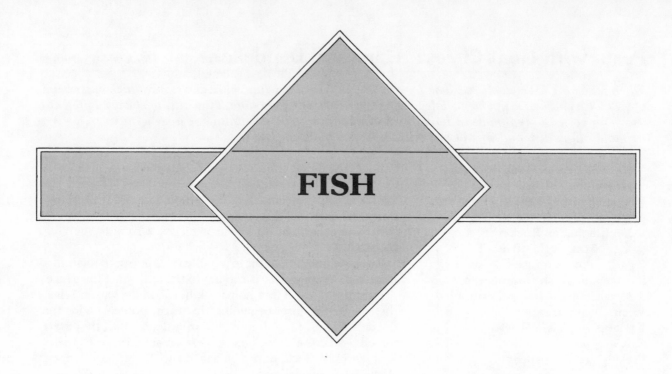

FISH

Sole Meunière

Makes 4 servings

Here are a few tips for making this into a very successful dish. Dip the sole filets in flour at the very last minute so they do not get soggy; the butter should be very hot when you sauté; be sure to turn the filets with a wide, flat spatula so that they do not fall apart; and serve them on heated dinner plates so that they stay piping hot and delicious. Garnish the plates with steamed parslied potatoes and a vegetable puree such as carrot. A chilled Chablis is the perfect accompaniment to this classic, simple dish.

1½ pounds filets of sole
¼ cup milk
6 tablespoons butter
¼ cup flour
1 tablespoon parsley, minced
4 lemon wedges

Cut the sole filets in half, perpendicular to the vertical axis, so that they are easier to handle when you turn them. Soak them in milk.

Place 2 tablespoons of the butter in a small skillet, off the heat.

Melt the remaining butter in a medium to large skillet, over low heat. When butter is melting, dip the sole filets in flour and shake off the excess. When the butter is very hot and turning golden, sauté the fish about 1 to 2 minutes per side, depending on how thick they are. Turn them over with a spatula.

As the fish is cooking on the second side, heat the 2 tablespoons of butter in the small skillet until the butter turns a nut brown. Remove the cooked fish to heated dinner plates, pour the nut-brown butter over it, and garnish with the minced parsley.

Serve with lemon wedges.

Baked Oriental Salmon

Makes 4 servings

These are baked salmon steaks lightly seasoned with a sauce of Mirin (a sweet rice wine mixture), soy sauce and rice vinegar. This sauce, often used when grilling or broiling fish, also works extremely well as a marinade.

4 tablespoons soy sauce
4 tablespoons Mirin
4 tablespoons rice vinegar
½ teaspoon sugar
4 6-ounce salmon steaks
1 scallion, green part included,
   thinly sliced
Salt
Freshly ground pepper

Preheat the oven to 400 degrees.

Mix together the soy sauce, Mirin, rice vinegar, sugar, ½ teaspoon salt and ¼ teaspoon pepper. Marinate the salmon steaks in this mixture for about 30 minutes, turning the salmon occasionally.

Drain the salmon steaks and pat them dry, reserving the marinade. Place them in a baking dish and bake for 25 minutes, or until the salmon is just cooked. Five minutes before the salmon is due to come out of the oven, start to boil the marinade in a small skillet over medium heat until it is reduced to ¼ cup in all. Stir in half the sliced scallion.

To serve, place a salmon steak on each warmed dinner plate and spoon some reduced sauce over it; garnish each portion with sliced scallion.

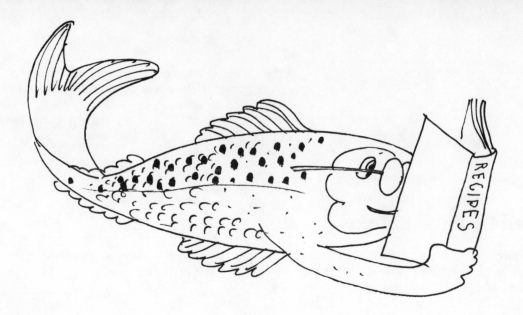

Stuffed Sole

Makes 4 servings

The flavors of this stuffing are simple and appealing. This is one of the most popular recipes I teach in my cooking school because it is easy and can be done in advance. Do not restrict yourself to stuffing sole with this mixture; it works well also in baked tomatoes and in hollowed-out zucchini boats. As a side dish, you could serve either the Peas with Lettuce and Cream or Stir-Fried Watercress and Carrots, and a Chablis would be a fine choice for the wine.

4 tablespoons olive oil
1 small onion, finely chopped
1 small carrot, finely chopped
½ pound shrimp, peeled and
    deveined
¼ cup heavy cream
1 tablespoon lemon juice
½ teaspoon dried tarragon
¼ cup fresh breadcrumbs
1 tablespoon butter
1½ pounds filets of sole
Salt
Freshly ground pepper

Preheat oven to 375 degrees.

Heat 3 tablespoons of the olive oil in a 9-inch skillet. When hot, add onion and carrot. Cover and cook for 10 minutes or until soft. Remove cover, add the shrimp and sauté for a couple of minutes, or until shrimp are pink and firm to the touch.

Remove mixture to a food processor and blend with the heavy cream, lemon juice, tarragon and breadcrumbs until mixture is pureed. Season with ½ teaspoon salt and ¼ teaspoon pepper.

With the tablespoon of butter, lightly grease a large baking dish. Place some stuffing on one half of each sole filet. Fold the other half over the stuffing and transfer the filet to the baking dish. Dribble the remaining tablespoon of olive oil over the filets; season lightly with salt and pepper.*

Bake, covered, for 20 to 25 minutes, or until the flesh is cooked through and white, and the stuffing is hot.

Bluefish with Fennel and Tomato Sauce

Makes 4 servings

An extra benefit of this dish, apart from the fact that it tastes so good, is that you get two recipes for one, because you can use the fennel and tomato mixture as a vegetable accompaniment. The baking time will vary according to the thickness of the fish; count about ten minutes per inch of thickness, plus five minutes because fish is covered. Serve it with buttered brown rice and the Sautéed Escarole and Pancetta, accompanied by a Beaujolais Nouveau.

1½ pounds boneless, skinless
    bluefish filets
1 pound fresh fennel
5 tablespoons butter
1 tablespoon olive oil
2 medium-size garlic cloves, minced
1-inch strip of orange peel
½ teaspoon dry fennel seeds
¼ cup Pernod
1 cup peeled and drained canned
    tomatoes
Salt
Freshly ground pepper

Preheat oven to 375 degrees.

With 1 tablespoon of butter, lightly grease a baking dish large enough to accommodate all the fish filets in one layer. Season the filets lightly with salt and pepper and place them in the buttered baking dish.

Discard the feathery green tops of the fennel and cut the bulb into 1-inch pieces.

Melt 2 tablespoons of the butter with the olive oil in a 9-inch skillet. When hot, add the fresh fennel, garlic, orange peel, dried fennel, Pernod, ¾ teaspoon salt and ¼ teaspoon pepper. Cover and simmer, over medium heat, for 10 minutes.

Then add the tomatoes to the skillet and simmer, covered, for 10 minutes more. Remove the cover. If a lot of liquid remains in the skillet, evaporate it over high heat until the mixture looks syrupy. Remove the orange peel. Turn the heat off and stir in 2 tablespoons of butter. Adjust the seasoning. Spoon the mixture over fish. Cover with foil* and bake for 15 to 20 minutes depending on the thickness of the fish. Do not overbake, or it will be dry.

Pot au Feu de Mer

If you use a couple of convenience foods such as clam juice (without preservatives) and frozen spinach, this dish can be ready in an hour. It tastes even better made with fresh spinach and fish stock, but that would add a time dimension to your work which you may not want. Substitute another firm-fleshed fish such as swordfish if you cannot find fresh salmon. Have the fishmonger filet the fish for you to save time. Ask him to leave on the skin, because this helps to prevent the fish chunks from falling apart.

1 medium-size onion, chopped
½ cup dry white wine
½ cup white wine vinegar
1½ cups clam juice or fish stock
1 cup tomato juice
½ cup heavy cream
¼ teaspoon saffron
1 cup (6 ounces) white turnips, cut
 into ¼-inch julienne strips
2 carrots (4 ounces) sliced into
 ⅛-inch rounds
1 cup snow peas, halved
1 cup mushroom caps, sliced
1 cup spinach, thawed and drained
½ pound boneless salmon filets,
 cut into 1½-inch chunks
¾ pound boneless red snapper
 filets, cut into 1½-inch chunks
¾ pound boneless lemon sole filets,
 cut into 1½-inch chunks
12 oysters, shucked, with oyster
 liquor
2 tablespoons fresh dill, minced
¼ pound butter
Salt
Freshly ground pepper

Process the chopped onion with the wine and vinegar in a blender or food processor until pureed.

Reduce the white wine, onion and vinegar in a 6-quart saucepan, over medium heat, until the onion is almost completely dry. Add the clam juice, tomato juice and heavy cream and bring to a boil. Add saffron, 1 teaspoon salt and ¼ teaspoon pepper.

Add the turnips and carrots, and simmer for 3 minutes; add the snow peas, mushroom caps and spinach, and simmer for 2 minutes. Add the salmon and simmer for 2 minutes after the liquid comes back to a boil; then add the remaining fish and cook for another couple of minutes, after the liquid comes back to a simmer. Stir in the oysters and dill and gradually whisk in the butter, tablespoon by tablespoon until it all has melted in. Taste and adjust the seasoning.

To serve, ladle into deep soup bowls along with the liquid.

Scallops in Leek Beurre Blanc

The only tricky part to this recipe is whisking the butter into the leeks as swiftly as possible to prevent the sauce from separating. Serve this dish with lightly steamed zucchini, along with a dry white wine such as a Chardonnay. (By the way, the vivid colors of raw radishes and leeks are pleasantly muted by the cooking process.)

1 pound sea scallops
6 radishes, washed and thinly sliced
3 medium-size leeks
Grated rind of 1 lime
1½ cups water
¼ cup lime juice
½ cup milk
12 tablespoons butter, cold, cut into
   1-inch pieces
Salt
Freshly ground white pepper

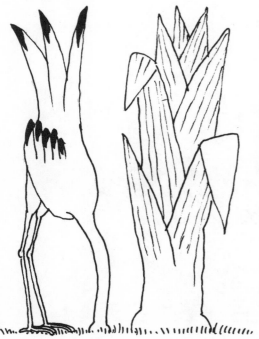

Remove and discard the small silvery protuberances on the sides of each scallop. Wash the scallops and pat them dry. Cut each one, horizontally, in two, to create ¼-inch circles. Toss them with the radishes, and set aside in the refrigerator.

Cut off the root end of the leeks and discard. Trim off all but 1½ inches of the leeks' green stems. Make two vertical cuts which criss-cross at right angles to each other, from the stem end down to 1 inch from the root end. Wash the leeks thoroughly under cold running water, making sure each section is free of sand. Then cut the leeks into cross pieces, about ½ inch wide.

Place the leeks, with the lime rind and 1 cup of the water, in a heavy 2-quart saucepan. Cover, bring to a boil, and simmer for 10 minutes. Remove the cover, add the lime juice, ¾ teaspoon salt and ¼ teaspoon pepper, and cook until the liquid has evaporated. Turn the heat off.*

Put the scallops and radishes in a 9-inch skillet. Cover with the remaining ½ cup water and the milk. Slowly bring the liquids to a boil, then simmer for 1 minute. Turn off the heat and cover to keep warm. Turn the heat on again under the leeks. Whisk in the cold butter, tablespoon by tablespoon, making sure to add a new piece only after the last one melts. Work fast so that the sauce does not separate. Adjust the seasoning.

To serve, drain the scallops and radishes and pat them dry. Add them to the sauce and toss the two together.

Scallop and Shrimp Pilaf

Makes 6 servings

There are so many ingredients in this dish that you can easily turn it into a complete meal by serving a steamed fresh green vegetable on the side. Also serve hot crusty French bread and a bottle of chilled Sauvignon Blanc.

1 pound sea scallops
1 cup tomato juice
1 cup clam juice or fish stock
Grated rind of 1 lemon
3 tablespoons lemon juice
6 tablespoons butter
2 medium-size onions, thinly sliced
½ teaspoon garlic, minced
1 cup long-grain white rice,
   uncooked
¾ pound shrimp, peeled and
   deveined
3 tablespoons fresh coriander leaves
   or fresh dill, minced
Salt
Freshly ground pepper

Slice each scallop into 3 horizontal rounds. Set aside, in the refrigerator.

Add the tomato juice to the clam juice with the lemon rind and juice, 1 teaspoon salt and ¼ teaspoon pepper.

Melt the butter in a 4-quart heavy saucepan. When it is hot, add the onions and garlic and simmer for 10 minutes, or until the onions are very soft and golden. Stir in the rice and sauté for about a minute more.* Add the clam and tomato juice mixture. Bring to a boil and simmer, covered, over low heat, for 12 minutes. Check every now and then to make sure the bottom is not burning. Add the scallops, shrimp, and coriander on top of the rice. Cover, and cook for another 5 minutes, or until the shrimp are pink and the scallops turn white. Stir the fish and coriander into the rice and adjust the seasoning.

POULTRY

Baked Chicken Thighs

Makes 4 servings

Accompany this dish with Broccoli with Lemon Butter Sauce, sautéed cherry tomatoes or a vegetable puree such as chick pea. Serve a light, fresh wine such as a Beaujolais Nouveau.

8 chicken thighs
5 tablespoons butter
1 tablespoon prepared mustard
¾ cup fresh breadcrumbs
½ cup Parmesan cheese, grated
2 tablespoons parsley, minced
Salt
Freshy ground pepper

Preheat oven to 400 degrees.

Lightly butter a 9-by-13-inch baking dish.

Melt the butter in a small skillet. Remove the butter from heat and mix in the mustard.

On a plate combine the breadcrumbs, Parmesan and parsley with salt and pepper. Dip the chicken thighs in the butter-and-mustard mixture, then pat the crumb mixture on the outside. Place the thighs in the baking pan and bake for 45 minutes.

NOTE: You may, of course, use legs with the thighs, but they may take a little longer to cook. Breadcrumbs made from rye bread or sourdough add a pleasant touch.

Chicken Packets Stuffed with Fontina

The Italian Fontina cheese has a low melting point, and this makes for a lovely, smooth filling. Shred the Fontina with a hand-held mouli grater, or do this on the large holes of a hand-held grater or in a food processor. It is easier to do when the cheese is cold. Serve this dish with the Stir-Fried Watercress and Carrots, buttered brown rice, and a dry white wine such as a Chardonnay.

4 whole chicken breasts, boned and skinned
½ pound Fontina cheese, finely shredded
¼ cup flour
4 tablespoons butter
⅔ cup dry white wine
¼ cup parsley, minced
Salt
Freshly ground pepper

Cut the chicken breasts in half along the line left by the breastbone. Trim off excess yellow fat. Pound the chicken between wax paper until it is about ¼ inch thick. Season both sides lightly with salt and pepper.

Place a portion of cheese in the center of each chicken piece and roll it up into a neat little packet. Try to enclose the cheese as much as possible. Fasten the packet with a toothpick or two.*

Dip the packets in flour and shake off excess. Heat 3 tablespoons of butter in a 12-inch skillet. Brown the chicken, on all sides, until golden. Add the wine and season with salt and pepper. Cover, and cook over low heat for 5 minutes. Remove cover and continue to cook for about 5 minutes more, uncovered. At this point, some of the cheese may ooze out. This is fine; it helps thicken the sauce. Stir in the remaining tablespoon of butter. Add parsley and serve 2 packets per person.

Gingered Barbecued Chicken Breasts

Makes 6 servings

This is wonderfully tasty, considering how easy it is to make. If you cannot get fresh ginger, then add more mustard to give it the appropriate bite; do not substitute powdered ginger. As a side dish, serve the Potato Sauté or the French-Fried Sweet Potatoes, along with lightly buttered broccoli or green beans. With this meal, I would serve a dark beer instead of wine.

½ cup ketchup
3 tablespoons Worcestershire sauce
2 tablespoons peanut oil
1 tablespoon honey
1½ teaspoons grated fresh ginger
1 teaspoon garlic, minced
½ teaspoon dry mustard
½ teaspoon chili powder
3 1-pound chicken breasts, on the bone
Salt
Freshly ground pepper

Preheat oven to 350 degrees.

Whisk all the ingredients except the chicken breasts together and season with ½ teaspoon salt and ¼ teaspoon pepper.

Place the chicken breasts in a baking pan, skin side up, and brush half the amount of sauce on the skins. Bake for 20 minutes. Brush the remaining sauce on the skins and bake for 20 minutes more.

To serve: with poultry shears or a very sharp knife, split the chicken breasts down the middle and serve one half of a breast per person.

Soy-Glazed Chicken Strips

Makes 4 servings

You could accompany this slightly Oriental chicken dish with any number of vegetable garnishes. I would serve either the Chick Pea Puree and the Zucchini with Dill, or the Fennel and Celery Knob Puree along with the Swiss Chard with Pear. I would drink Japanese or Chinese beer with this meal.

1½ pounds boneless, skinless chicken breasts
3 tablespoons sesame oil
3 tablespoons soy sauce
¼ cup rice vinegar
¼ teaspoon grated orange rind
1 teaspoon honey
Salt
Freshly ground pepper

Cut the chicken breasts into strips, approximately 6 inches by 1½ inches.

Heat the sesame oil in a large skillet, until hot. Add the chicken strips and sauté them for about 2½ minutes per side. Remove the chicken to a plate. Add soy sauce, vinegar, orange rind, and honey to the skillet and stir the mixture together.

Over high heat, reduce this sauce for a couple of minutes, or until it looks shiny and syrupy. Return the chicken strips to the sauce and heat them through for a minute or so. Taste for seasoning and adjust, before serving.

Quick Chicken Vallée D'Auge

Makes 4 servings

The curry powder adds color to the sauce; it does not change the flavor of the chicken. Serve this dish with egg noodles and steamed green beans. A refreshing wine accompaniment is hard cider.

1½ pounds boned chicken breasts
2 tart apples, peeled and grated
4 tablespoons butter
¼ cup flour
¼ cup onion, finely chopped
1 clove garlic, minced
⅛ teaspoon curry powder
2 tablespoons Calvados or applejack
¼ cup hard cider
¾ cup heavy cream
Salt
Freshly ground pepper

Cut the chicken breasts into strips, approximately 6 inches by ½ inch wide. Squeeze the apples to extract the juice. Reserve the apples (drink the juice, please; do not throw it out).

Melt the butter in a large skillet. Dip the chicken strips in flour and shake off excess. Sauté the chicken strips for about a minute per side, over medium to high heat. Remove the strips to a plate.

Add the onion and garlic to the skillet and sauté for a couple of minutes, or until the onion is soft. Add the curry powder, Calvados, cider and apples. Reduce the liquids by stirring over high heat until the apples are nearly dry. Add heavy cream and reduce for about 1 minute. Season with salt and pepper to taste. Return the chicken to the cream and apples and simmer them for about 3 minutes per side. Be sure to leave the skillet uncovered so that the cream continues to thicken as the chicken cooks through.

Cornish Game Hens, Baked with Boursin

Makes 4 servings

If you think that one hen per person is too generous a portion, just cut the recipe in half to serve four people. I, however, think it is so good that most people will want to eat a whole hen. With this, I would serve the Escarole with Pancetta and a bulgur wheat dish, along with a Zinfandel wine.

4 cornish game hens
1 Boursin cheese, with herbs
6 tablespoons butter, at room temperature
2 tablespoons lemon juice
1 egg yolk
Salt
Freshly ground pepper

Preheat oven to 375 degrees.

With poultry shears, or a sharp knife, cut along one side of the backbone of each hen, then alongside the other, in order to remove the backbone entirely. Flatten out the hens and place them, skin side up, in one or two baking pans, depending on their size.

Beat the Boursin cheese with the butter until blended. Beat in the lemon juice and season with salt and pepper.

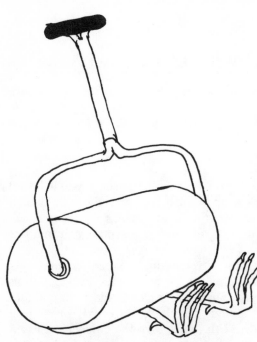

Spread half of this mixture on the skins of the hens, and bake them for 25 minutes. Meanwhile, beat the egg yolk into the remaining cheese-and-butter mixture and reserve until later. After 25 minutes, remove the hens from the oven and spread the cheese-and-yolk mixture all over the skins. Bake for 20 minutes more.

To serve, remove the hens from the baking pan to a platter or to individual serving plates, and spoon over them any butter and cheese that has melted in the baking pan.

Sesame Chicken Salad

Makes 6 servings

This was inspired by a well-known Chinese dish known as cold noodles with sesame oil. The exotic flavors, combined with mayonnaise, make a terrific dressing for chicken salad. I like to add the dressing to the chicken when it is still warm, so that the meat absorbs more of the flavors of the dressing. The sesame paste and rice vinegar can be bought in Oriental or health food stores.

**3 large, whole chicken breasts
   (1 pound each)
6 tablespoons peanut butter
2 tablespoons sesame paste
½ cup mayonnaise
3 tablespoons soy sauce
4 tablespoons rice vinegar
2 garlic cloves, minced
Lettuce leaves, washed
2 scallions, with 2 inches of green
   stem left on, sliced thinly
Salt
Freshly ground pepper**

Place the chicken breasts in cold water in a 4-quart pot. The water should cover the chicken breasts. Slowly bring the water to a boil and poach the chicken breasts at a bare simmer for 5 minutes. Cool the chicken in water for 15 minutes. Remove from the water. Tear off the skin and separate the meat from the bones. Shred the chicken into pieces about 2 inches by 1 inch.

Combine the peanut butter, sesame paste, mayonnaise, soy sauce, vinegar, and garlic in a blender or food processor. Season with 1 teaspoon salt and ¼ teaspoon pepper. Taste and adjust the seasoning.

Combine the dressing with the chicken and serve immediately, or marinate for 2 hours.*

To serve, place the chicken salad on lettuce leaves and garnish with sliced scallions.

Boneless Chicken Breasts, Deglazed with Lime   *Makes 4 servings*

Be sure to sauté the chicken over fairly high heat to sear in the juices and form a firm crust. Fresh coriander is readily available in Oriental produce markets, but if you cannot find it, you may substitute parsley. The flavor, though, will not be as interesting. You will notice that I detach the filets from the breast and reserve them for another use. That is so that the chicken breasts are all the same thickness and will cook at an even rate.

1½ pounds boneless chicken breasts
3 tablespoons flour
2 teaspoons oregano
2 tablespoons vegetable oil
1 tablespoon butter
Grated rind of 1 medium-size lime
Grated rind of 1 medium-size lemon
¼ cup water
2 tablespoons each of lime and lemon juice
2 tablespoons fresh coriander, finely chopped
Salt
Freshly ground pepper

On the underside of each half chicken breast, you will find an easily detachable strip of meat known as the filet. Detach it and save it to use in another dish, such as a chicken salad.

Combine the flour, oregano and ½ teaspoon salt in a flat dish. Set aside.

Heat the oil and butter in a 10-inch skillet. As this heats up, dip each piece of chicken, on both sides, into the flour-and-oregano mixture. Shake off excess. Add to the skillet and sauté, without moving the chicken around, for about 2 minutes on one side. With tongs, turn the chicken over and sauté for another 2 to 3 minutes. Remove the chicken to a plate and keep warm. (If all the chicken did not fit into the skillet, then sauté the second batch as you did the first.)

Turn the heat off under skillet. Add the citrus rinds and juices along with ¼ cup water. Be careful, as you do this, as it steams up furiously. Return the skillet to the heat and deglaze the drippings into the juices. Reduce this for about 30 seconds over high heat, or until it looks syrupy. Add the coriander and season to taste with salt and pepper. Spoon the sauce over the chicken.

Stuffed Boneless Turkey Breasts

This stuffing would be fine for a whole turkey but because this recipe makes only half a cup of stuffing, you would have to increase the volume substantially. Serve a colorful side dish such as the Sautéed Watercress with Carrots, or steamed broccoli; serve a Sauvignon Blanc wine along with it.

4 tablespoons butter
1 cup (6 ounces) onions, finely chopped
2 tablespoons smoked oysters or clams, chopped
½ cup pecans, ground
½ cup heavy cream
1½ pounds boneless, skinless turkey cutlets, cut from the breast
Salt
Freshly ground white pepper

Heat 2 tablespoons of butter in a small skillet. Add the onions and smoked oysters and sauté for 1 minute. Cover and simmer, over low heat, for about 10 minutes, or until the onions are translucent. Uncover the skillet and add the pecans; season with ¼ teaspoon salt and ¼ teaspoon pepper. Add ¼ cup of the heavy cream and keep this warm over very low heat or over a flame tamer.

Heat the remaining 2 tablespoons of butter in a 12-inch skillet. When hot, sauté turkey cutlets for about 2 to 3 minutes per side, over medium-high heat. They are done when they are no longer pink inside; however, they should remain moist. Season lightly with salt and pepper and remove to a plate to keep them warm.

Deglaze the skillet with the remaining heavy cream. Turn off the heat and season lightly with salt and pepper.

To serve, center the turkey on warm dinner plates; spoon the stuffing underneath each cutlet and spoon some of the sauce on top.

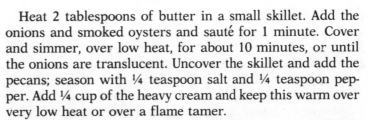

Sauté of Chicken Livers, Bacon and Apples

Do not stir the chicken livers around as you sauté them; this prevents the development of the crisp, firm outside crust which is an agreeable characteristic of this dish. Serve with bulgur wheat and a sauté of spinach along with a fresh, fruity wine such as Chenin Blanc.

1½ pounds chicken livers
6 slices bacon, finely diced
2 tablespoons butter
2 tablespoons shallots, finely chopped
¾ cup tart apples, finely diced
3 tablespoons Calvados or applejack
6 tablespoons heavy cream
1 tablespoon parsley, minced

Examine the chicken livers and carefully remove fat and any bright green spots which you may find. Wash and pat dry.

Sauté the bacon with 1 tablespoon of butter in a 10-inch skillet, until the bacon fat has rendered out. With a slotted spoon, remove the bacon bits and reserve until later. In the remaining bacon fat, sauté the chicken livers over high heat, in 2 batches, for about 2 minutes per side. (As you do this, avert your face and do not stay near the skillet because chicken livers over heat spatter wildly.) Remove the chicken livers to a plate and reserve until later.

Remove all but 1 tablespoon of the fat in the skillet. In this remaining fat, sauté the shallots until soft. Then add the apples, Calvados and heavy cream. With a wooden spoon, scrape up the browned particles in bottom of pan and incorporate them into the liquids.*

Return the chicken livers and bacon to the simmering cream and cook them for about 3 minutes more, keeping the heat low so that they do not toughen. Turn the heat off. Adjust the seasoning. Whisk in the last tablespoon of butter. Transfer the livers to a serving dish, and dust with parsley before serving.

MEAT

Lamb Steaks

Makes 4 servings

The sauce is a cold, spicy vinaigrette, somewhat like a parsley sauce, which is served in Argentina with grilled meats. Along with this dish you could serve the French-Fried Sweet Potatoes, steamed green beans, and a bottle of red Gamay to round out the meal.

¼ cup olive oil
3 tablespoons red wine vinegar
3 tablespoons onion, finely
   chopped
½ cup parsley, chopped
½ teaspoon prepared mustard
½ teaspoon oregano
½ teaspoon chili powder
1 tablespoon olive oil
4 12-ounce lamb steaks, cut from
   the leg, each one about 1 inch
   thick
Salt
Freshly ground pepper

Combine the ¼ cup olive oil, vinegar, onion, parsley, mustard, oregano, chili powder, ½ teaspoon salt and ¼ teaspoon pepper and set aside.

Heat the remaining tablespoon olive oil in a 12-inch skillet. Sauté the lamb steaks over high heat for about 5 minutes per side. Season lightly with salt and pepper.

Serve each steak on heated dinner plates; ladle some sauce on each portion and then serve the remainder on the side.

Pan-Broiled Skirt Steaks

Makes 4 servings

Skirt steaks, which come from the underside of beef, are more flavorful and cheaper than are more tender, expensive cuts of meat such as filet mignon. You can also use flank steak, but you'll have to cook it for a couple of minutes longer because it is a thicker cut. Pan-broiling the steaks produces so much smoke that you should not do this recipe without opening the windows wide or turning on the exhaust fan. If you do not heed this admonition, your neighbors will undoubtedly call the fire department!

1½ pounds trimmed skirt steaks
1 tablespoon coarsely cracked
   peppercorns
1 tablespoon shallots, finely
   chopped
2 tablespoons brandy
½ cup heavy cream
Coarse salt

Trim the steaks of just about all traces of fat. Press peppercorns into both sides.

Sprinkle 1½ teaspoons of coarse salt in a 10-inch skillet. Heat the skillet until very hot and pan-broil the steaks, 3 minutes per side. Remove the steaks to a cutting board.

Add the shallots, 2 tablespoons water and brandy to the skillet. The mixture will steam furiously at this point because the pan is so hot. Add the heavy cream and reduce for a couple of minutes, or until the sauce is thick. If the steaks give off juice while resting on the cutting board, add this to the sauce and reduce further if necessary. Taste for seasoning and adjust.

To serve, slice the steaks across the grain into ½-inch-thick slices and spoon some sauce over them.

Spicy Sausages with Pears

The pear is a sweet accent for the robust, garlicky sausage, but apples would do equally well. To round out the menu, serve the Egg and Vegetable Salad as a first course, mashed potatoes and Brussels Sprouts in Walnut Butter as side dishes, along with an assertive red wine or dark beer.

2 pounds Italian spicy-and-hot pork sausages
4 medium-size Bosc pears, peeled, cored and sliced into ½-inch pieces
Red wine

Place the sausages in a 12-inch skillet with ½ inch of red wine. Cover and simmer for 15 minutes. Remove the cover and continue to cook, sautéeing sausages in their own fat, to create a crusty exterior. Sauté them for about 20 minutes more, turning them frequently.

Discard all but 1 tablespoon of fat from the skillet. Add the pears, cover, and cook for 5 minutes more or until pears are just tender.

To serve, spoon the sausages along with the pears on each dish.

Veal Scaloppini Breaded with Parmesan

There are three rules to remember when making this dish. Chill the breaded veal to set the coating; let the fat get very hot so that the coating sizzles and immediately forms a crust; most importantly, do not move the veal around in skillet until each side forms a crust. Moving the veal just dislodges the breading. Serve this dish with the Celery Knob Puree and Broccoli with Lemon Butter.

1½ pounds veal scaloppini
⅓ cup flour lightly seasoned with salt and pepper
1 egg beaten with 1 tablespoon water
2 cups freshly made breadcrumbs mixed with ½ cup grated Parmesan cheese
6 tablespoons olive oil

Preheat oven to 250 degrees.

If the butcher has not pounded the meat, then do so, in between wax paper, using a mallet or pounder, until the slices are ¼ inch thick.

Dip each piece in flour, then in egg and then pat breadcrumbs and Parmesan on both sides. Put the coated veal pieces on cookie racks, and place in the refrigerator; leave for half an hour.*

Just before serving, heat the olive oil in a large skillet until it is very hot. Sauté the veal, over medium-high heat, for about 1½ minutes. With a flat metal spatula, turn the veal over and sauté for another 1½ minutes. You will have to do this in 2 or 3 batches or until all the veal is cooked. As you finish a batch, keep it warm, uncovered, in the preheated low oven.

Stuffed Veal Bundles

Makes 4 servings

To shape an entire menu around the veal, first serve Mushrooms Stuffed with Parsley-Garlic Butter. Accompany the veal with the Celery Knob and Fennel Puree, along with a sauté of carrots and a Chardonnay. End the meal with the Hazelnut Chocolate Pôts de Crème.

1 8-ounce zucchini, cut into ¼-inch dice
½ cup frozen peas, thawed
1 scallion, with the green top left on
2 ounces cream cheese
1½ pounds veal scaloppini, pounded to ¼-inch thickness
3 tablespoons butter
3 tablespoon lemon juice
½ teaspoon dry oregano
Salt
Freshly ground pepper

Parboil the zucchini for 1½ minutes. Drain and cool.

Puree the peas, scallion and cream cheese in a blender or food processor. Season with ¼ teaspoon salt and ¼ teaspoon pepper. Stir the diced zucchini into this mixture and set aside.

Spoon about 2 tablespoons of the mixture into each veal scaloppine, roll it up, and fasten each bundle with a toothpick.*

Melt the butter over high heat in a 12-inch skillet. Sear the veal bundles for 1 minute per side, over high heat. Lower the heat, cover the skillet and simmer for 3 minutes. Remove the veal bundles to a plate. Add lemon juice and oregano to the skillet and scrape up the coagulated juices into the liquids. Reduce the sauce by half. Season with salt and pepper. Remove the toothpicks from veal; serve 2 veal bundles per person and spoon some of the sauce over each bundle.

Pork Chops with Mustard Sauerkraut

Makes 4 servings

Never overcook pork or it will dry out and lose its fine, delicate flavor. A carrot or sweet potato puree is an attractive and good-tasting side dish to serve with this pork recipe, and either beer or a Cabernet Sauvignon would go well with it.

4 loin pork chops, 1-inch thick
2 cups sauerkraut, rinsed and squeezed dry
2 teaspoons prepared mustard
½ cup heavy cream
4 teaspoons brown sugar
4 tablespoons seasoned flour
2 tablespoons vegetable oil
Salt
Freshly ground pepper

Preheat oven to 375 degrees.

Trim as much of the outside fat from the loin pork chops as you can.

Combine the sauerkraut, mustard, cream, sugar and salt and pepper. Place this mixture on the bottom of a baking dish large enough to accommodate the chops in one layer.

Dip the pork chops in the seasoned flour and shake off the excess very thoroughly.

Heat the oil in a 12-inch skillet. When hot, sauté the chops, over medium heat, for about 2 to 3 minutes per side or until

they have developed a firm, golden crust. Season the chops lightly with salt and pepper and place them on top of the sauerkraut.

Bake, uncovered, for 20 minutes more.

To serve, center a pork chop on each dinner plate and serve the sauerkraut on the side.

Lamb with Feta and Tomatoes

Makes 4 servings

Serve this with the Cumin Brown Rice recipe or the Swiss Chard with Pear. A Zinfandel would be a good accompaniment. You could serve the Spicy Peanut Soup as a first course and the Pear Brown Betty to make a complete meal.

8 6-ounce loin lamb chops, about
   1½ inches thick
3 tablespoons flour seasoned with
   salt and pepper
3 tablespoons olive oil
1 medium-size onion, finely
   chopped
1 clove garlic, minced
1 cup peeled, seeded and drained
   canned tomatoes
3 tablespoons lemon juice
½ teaspoon oregano
¼ teaspoon anise seeds
½ cup feta cheese, crumbled
Salt
Freshly ground pepper

Preheat oven to 375 degrees.

Trim the lamb chops of some of their outside fat. Dip them lightly in the seasoned flour and shake off excess.

Heat 1 tablespoon of the olive oil in a 12-inch skillet. When it is hot, add the lamb chops and sear, over medium-high heat, for 3 minutes per side. Remove the chops to a baking dish large enough to accommodate all the lamb chops in one layer. Bake for about 15 minutes for medium-rare lamb, or longer if you like your chops well done.

Discard all the fat from the skillet. Add the remaining 2 tablespoons of olive oil. Sauté the onion and garlic for a couple of minutes or until soft. Add the tomatoes, lemon juice, oregano and anise and simmer, uncovered, until the lamb chops are done. At the very last minute, whisk in the feta cheese and stir until all the cheese is dissolved. Season with salt and pepper. Serve the sauce over the lamb chops.

Medallions of Lamb with Mustard Béarnaise

Makes 4 servings

Reserve this dish for special occasions because it is rather costly to make and the sauce, a variation on the béarnaise theme, is rich and festive. Precede it with a light broth or consommé. Serve sautéed cherry tomatoes or a steamed green vegetable as garnish and follow that with a salad course and the Chocolate Soufflés. A Cabernet Sauvignon would be my choice of wine.

1 teaspoon prepared mustard
1 tablespoon tomato paste
1½ pounds boned loin of lamb, in one piece
2 tablespoons shallots, finely chopped
⅓ cup red wine vinegar
⅓ cup red wine
1 tablespoon dried tarragon
3 egg yolks, at room temperature
12 tablespoons butter, cut into 1-inch pieces, chilled
Salt
Freshly ground pepper

Mix the mustard and tomato paste with 1 tablespoon of water. Set aside.

With a sharp knife, remove all the thick, hard white fat surrounding the meat. Cut the loin into cross pieces about 1 inch thick. Season lightly with salt and pepper.* Place the lamb in a stainless steel colander that will fit into a wider pan. Place about 1 inch of water into that wide pan and bring it to a boil, *without* the lamb.

While the water is coming to a boil, reduce the shallots, vinegar, wine and tarragon over high heat until the liquid is almost completely evaporated and the mixture looks syrupy. Remove from the heat.

When the water comes to a boil, place the colander containing the lamb in the pot. Cover the pot and steam, over low heat, for about 4 minutes. Meanwhile, finish the sauce.

Add the egg yolks to the tarragon mixture and whisk over low heat until the yolks look sticky. Add the butter, one piece at a time, whisking non-stop until all the butter is incorporated. The minute all the butter is in, remove the sauce from the heat and adjust the seasoning. Whisk in the mustard and tomato paste. It is all right to serve this sauce tepid. To serve, remove the lamb to a platter and pat it dry with towels. Spoon some sauce over it to mask its greyish color.

NOTE: It may seem odd to have included a delicate sauce in a book containing easy recipes. This is, in fact, an easy sauce to do, just as long as you use a saucepan that is heavy enough to prevent the eggs from scrambling.

Ham Steaks with Apple Sauce

I wonder whether the dessert we know as applesauce really started as a sauce to accompany meats. Whether it did or not, it certainly works well as a sauce for duck, ham or venison. The ham I use for this recipe is a prepared ham. If, however, your household is graced with a cured Smithfield ham, be sure to sauté the meat for five minutes more.

2 1-pound ham steaks, about ¾ inch thick
2 large apples (1 pound), cored, peeled and sliced thinly
¼ cup Armagnac or brandy
½ cup beef stock or water
¼ teaspoon dry mustard
¼ teaspoon mace
⅛ teaspoon ground cloves
1 tablespoon superfine sugar
½ cup raisins
6 tablespoons butter

Trim the fat and skin from the ham steaks.

Simmer the apples, Armagnac, stock, mustard, mace and cloves for 15 minutes or until the apples are soft. Puree them in a blender or food processor. Add the sugar and raisins and set aside.*

Sauté the ham steaks in a 10-inch skillet in 2 tablespoons butter for about 5 minutes per side. Remove the steaks to a platter and keep them warm.

Deglaze the skillet with the apple sauce and raisins, and season with salt and pepper. Whisk the remaining 4 tablespoons of butter into the sauce and adjust the seasoning.

To serve, center the ham in the middle of the plate, cut into serving pieces and spoon the apple sauce around the slices.

NOTE: You can broil the ham steaks instead of sautéeing them. If you do, then heat the sauce in a small skillet and whisk in the butter. You will have to trust me on the taste of the sauce. On its own, it misses the wonderful taste it has when combined with ham.

Steak Diane

This is my version of a fairly classic recipe, although there are few recipes around to prove that it is a standard. Ask your butcher to choose the most appropriate cut of steak for sautéeing. I use what is known as the "Delmonico" cut. Serve this with Glazed Turnips and the Sautéed Escarole with Pancetta.

4 8-ounce boneless steaks, "Delmonico" cut
2 teaspoons cracked black peppercorns
5 tablespoons butter
1 tablespoon oil
3 tablespoons shallots or onion, finely chopped
1 tablespoon red wine vinegar
1 tablespoon prepared mustard
½ cup beef stock or bouillon
1 tablespoon Worcestershire sauce
¼ cup Cognac or brandy
¼ cup parsley, minced

Remove the outside fat from the steaks and pound them, with a mallet or meat pounder, until they are about ½ inch thick. (You could also get your butcher to do that.) Press peppercorns into both sides.

Heat 1 tablespoon of the butter with the vegetable oil in a 12-inch skillet. Heat until very hot and then sauté the steaks for about 30 seconds on each side. Remove them to a platter.

Discard all but 1 tablespoon of fat. Add the shallots to the remaining fat and cook for 1 minute. Add the vinegar, mustard, stock, Worcestershire and Cognac and reduce for 2 to 3 minutes, or until thick and syrupy.* Whisk in the remaining 4 tablespoons of butter and parsley and stir until the butter has just melted. Add the steaks to the sauce and simmer them, over low heat, for 1 minute until they are just heated through. Season to taste with salt and pepper.

To serve, place each steak on a platter and ladle some sauce over it. Serve the remainder of the sauce on the side.

VEGETABLES

Broccoli with Lemon Butter

Makes 4 servings

The lemon sauce that accompanies the steamed broccoli in this recipe has a satiny quality because the water in it evaporates as the butter melts, which keeps the butter from separating.

1 bunch broccoli, cut into florets
Grated rind of 1 lemon
3 tablespoons lemon juice
¼ cup water
5 tablespoons butter, cut into
   tablespoon pieces
Salt
Freshly ground pepper

Bring 1 inch of water to a boil in a 4-quart saucepan. Place the steamer in the saucepan. Place the broccoli in the steamer. Cover, and cook for about 5 minutes or until it is tender, but has some crunch left in it.

While the broccoli is steaming, start the sauce. Combine the lemon rind, lemon juice and water in a 9-inch skillet. Bring this to a boil and reduce for a minute or so until these juices begin to thicken. When the broccoli is done, whisk the butter, tablespoon by tablespoon, and the frothing juices. When all the butter is in, continue to let the sauce cook, whisking all the while, for 30 seconds. Season to taste with salt and pepper.

Drain the broccoli, pat it dry with towels, and spoon the sauce over the broccoli.

Brussels Sprouts and Celery in Walnut Butter

Makes 4 servings

The very words "brussels sprouts" make most people wrinkle up their noses. This is, however, a perfectly lovely vegetable provided you do not overcook it. Here it is made more interesting by adding the diced celery and by sautéeing it in butter mixed with mustard and walnuts. The walnuts absorb the butter, making it adhere to the brussels sprouts. Serve this with roast beef, or roast chicken, along with a vegetable puree as another side dish.

1 pound brussels sprouts
2 celery stalks, finely diced
1 cup walnuts, finely chopped
6 tablespoons butter
1 tablespoon prepared mustard
  mixed with 1 tablespoon water
Salt
Freshly ground pepper

Trim the bottoms of the brussels sprouts and remove any brown or yellowish outer leaves. Cut each one in half.

Bring 1 inch of water to a boil in a 4-quart saucepan. Place a vegetable steamer in the pot. Add the brussels sprouts and celery and steam them, covered, for about 5 minutes or until just tender.

When the sprouts are just about cooked, heat the butter in a 9-inch skillet. When the butter turns light brown, add the steamed brussels sprouts and celery, the mustard mixed with water, and the walnuts. Season with ¼ teaspoon salt and ¼ teaspoon pepper. Sauté until just heated through, and serve at once.

Bulgur Wheat, Peppers and Bean Curd

Makes 4 servings

Although completely vegetarian, this meal is quite high in protein not only because of the protein in the bean curd but because the cheese and bean curd, in combination with the wheat, make a complementary protein. For even more nutrition, you can substitute brown rice for the cracked wheat. The color of the red peppers and green spinach makes for an attractive meatless meal, made in a single skillet.

1 cup bulgur wheat
2 fresh sweet red peppers, washed
½ pound fresh spinach
4 bean curd cakes, each about 3
  inches square and 1 inch thick
¼ pound sharp cheddar cheese
4 tablespoons butter
1 tablespoon garlic, minced
2 tablespoons cider vinegar
Salt
Freshly ground pepper

Place the bulgur wheat in a bowl. Bring 2 cups of water to a boil with ½ teaspoon salt. Pour this over the wheat and let wheat stand for 20 minutes, or long enough to absorb the water. After it has absorbed the water, drain off any excess thoroughly.

While the wheat is softening, prepare the remaining ingredients. Seed and julienne the red peppers into ¼-inch pieces; stem and wash the spinach; cut the bean curd cakes into ½-inch dice; grate the cheese.

Heat the butter in a 12-inch skillet until it is golden brown. Add the garlic and sauté for 30 seconds. Add the peppers, cover, and simmer for 5 minutes over medium heat. Remove the cover and add the drained wheat and vinegar. Stir for 5 minutes, without a cover. Add the bean curd and spinach; cover and simmer, over low heat, for about another 5 minutes or until the spinach has wilted.

Season very well with 1 teaspoon salt and ¼ teaspoon pepper. If you are too cautious at this point, the dish will taste flat. If you find the dish too moist, evaporate some of the excess water over medium heat. Stir in the cheese and remove the dish from heat when the cheese has just melted.

Chick Pea Puree with Lemon and Garlic
Makes 4-6 servings

Served with fresh spinach, this recipe makes a fine cold summer salad. To do so, use oil, instead of butter, when cooking the garlic, and thicken the puree with yogurt instead of heavy cream. Season it more heavily with salt and pepper, as cold tends to deaden the taste.

1-pound can chick peas, drained
2 tablespoons butter
1 teaspoon garlic, minced
¼ teaspoon grated lemon rind
¼ teaspoon grated orange rind
2 tablespoons lemon juice
¼ cup heavy cream
6 tablespoons parsley, minced
Salt
Freshly ground pepper

Puree the chick peas in a food mill or food processor.

Melt the butter in a small skillet. When it is half melted, add the garlic and sauté over low heat until all the butter is melted and the garlic emits a lovely aroma. Take care not to let the garlic burn, because this will ruin the flavor of the dish. Whisk the garlic and butter into the chick pea puree along with the other ingredients. Season with ¾ teaspoon salt and ¼ teaspoon pepper. You could also puree the complete recipe in a food processor.*

NOTE: To reheat, do so directly over heat, stirring constantly, or use a double boiler.

Celery Knob and Fennel Puree

Fall fennel and winter celery root naturally complement each other. The onions add flavor and the potatoes give body. This is an unusual accompaniment and works well with pork, lamb or venison. The color, however, is a bit dull, so be sure to brighten it with a sprinkling of parsley before presenting the dish at the table.

¼ pound butter
1 pound fennel, cleaned and sliced
1 medium-size onion, sliced
1-pound celery knob
1 large boiling potato
½ teaspoon dried thyme
½ cup heavy cream
1 tablespoon parsley, minced
Salt
Freshly ground white pepper

Melt the butter in a 4-quart saucepan. When it is hot, add the fennel and onion. Cover, and simmer over low heat.

While this is cooking, peel away the thick nubby skin from the celery knob. (Do this with a stainless steel knife, to prevent the celery from browning.) Chop it up roughly into 1-inch pieces and add to the fennel and onion.

Then peel the potato and dice it into small pieces. Add this to the saucepan with ½ cup water, thyme, 1½ teaspoons salt and ¼ teaspoon pepper. Cover, and simmer over low heat for 20 to 25 minutes, or until the vegetables are tender.

Drain the vegetables, transfer to a food processor or food mill and puree with the cream. Adjust the salt and pepper to taste.* Garnish with parsley and serve.

NOTE: If you do this in advance, you can reheat it in a double boiler. The puree freezes well.

Bulgur Wheat, Sautéed with Yogurt

Makes 4 servings

Bulgur wheat, which also goes by the name of tabbouleh, is readily available in health food stores, and in some supermarkets. It is a precooked grain with a mild nutty flavor. Remarkably easy to prepare, this recipe is a perfect foil for sauces and you might think of serving it instead of rice.

4 tablespoons butter
1 onion, finely chopped
2 celery stalks, finely chopped
1 cup bulgur wheat
1½ cups chicken stock, or water
2 tablespoons plain yogurt
2 tablespoons fresh parsley, minced
Salt
Freshly ground pepper

Heat the butter in a 9-inch skillet. When it is hot, add the onion and celery and sauté over medium heat for about 5 minutes, or until the onion is translucent.

Add the bulgur wheat and continue to sauté for 1 minute more. Add the stock, ½ teaspoon salt and ¼ teaspoon pepper. Cover, and simmer over low heat for 15 minutes or until the wheat is tender.* If it is not tender enough for your taste, just simmer it a bit longer. Taste for seasoning and adjust.

Turn the heat off and stir in the yogurt and parsley.

NOTE: To reheat the wheat, just heat it up in a little more butter or place it in a skillet with some water and steam it until it heats through. However, when you add water, the wheat will lose some of its crunch.

Cumin Brown Rice with Raisins

Makes 4-6 servings

Although making this dish does take a full hour, I decided to include it because brown rice is decidedly healthier than white rice and, in my opinion, tastes better too. Be sure to buy the long-grain type, which is now available in supermarkets, to avoid ending up with a mushy mess.

1 medium-size onion, finely sliced
3 tablespoons butter
½ teaspoon ground cumin
1 cup long-grain brown rice
1½ cups lightly seasoned chicken
   stock, or water
2-inch piece of cinnamon stick
2 tablespoons raisins or
   currants
Salt
Freshly ground pepper

Simmer the onion in the butter in a 2-quart saucepan over medium heat for about 5 minutes, or until translucent. Add the cumin and stir for 30 seconds. Add the rice, stock, cinnamon stick, ¾ teaspoon salt and ¼ teaspoon pepper. Bring the liquid to a boil, cut it back to a simmer and cook, covered, for 40 minutes. Remove the cover and stir in the raisins. Cook for 10 to 15 minutes longer, without the cover, to evaporate the liquid.

NOTE: The rice should still have some bite to it; it should not be completely soft. If you like it softer, however, cook it longer.

Glazed Turnips

Some people snub turnips, but this recipe might make converts. It goes beautifully with pork, duck and chicken.

1½ pounds white turnips, peeled
4 tablespoons butter
1 cup chicken or beef stock
2 tablespoons sugar
2 tablespoons parsley, minced
Salt
Freshly ground white pepper

Cut the turnips into quarters, or until you have formed pieces that are approximately 2 inches long and about 1 inch wide. Bring 2 quarts of water to a boil and boil the turnips for 3 minutes. Drain. This helps rid them of their pungent flavor.

Melt the butter in a 9-inch skillet. When it is hot, add the turnips, along with the stock and sugar, ½ teaspoon salt and ¼ teaspoon white pepper. Cover, and simmer over medium heat for 20 minutes or until tender.*

Remove the cover and reduce the liquid, over high heat, until it is dark and syrupy. Adjust the salt and pepper and sprinkle the top with parsley.

French-Fried Sweet Potatoes

The taste of sweet potato is immensely satisfying, and this vegetable is also high in vitamin A. The only problem with it is that it takes a long time to bake. When I have a yen for the taste of sweet potatoes, I cut them up and deep-fry them. The entire job is done in 30 minutes.

1 pound lard
2 cups peanut oil
1¼ pounds sweet potatoes
Coarse salt
Freshly ground pepper

Place the lard and peanut oil in a deep kettle with a flat bottom. Heat the fats to 375 degrees, measured on a deep-frying thermometer. As the oil and lard heat up, peel and cut the potatoes into approximately 2-by-¼-inch julienne strips.

When the fat is hot, fry the sweet potatoes for about 6 minutes.* Do this in several batches, depending on how wide your frying pot is. When the potatoes are fried, remove them to a grill, placed over paper to absorb any dripping fat. Season generously with a mixture of coarse salt and freshly ground pepper.

NOTE: If you cannot find lard, use about 1 quart of oil in all. However, the flavor of pork fat enhances that of the sweet potato sufficiently to make it worth your while to search for the lard.

Fresh Mustard Greens with Anchovy Sauce

Makes 4 servings

Mustard greens are an interesting vegetable. When raw, they are sharp and biting like mustard. When cooked, they have a milder yet distinctive flavor. Use bits of fresh raw mustard greens for a different taste in salads. Be sure to buy greens that have leaves no longer than 6 or 8 inches. Large, overgrown leaves inevitably mean the greens will be bitter, so pick greens as young and fresh as possible.

1½ pounds fresh mustard greens
¼ cup olive oil
1 teaspoon garlic, minced
4 anchovies, finely chopped
¼ cup black olives, preferably
   Niçoise type, pitted
1 tablespoon capers
¼ cup red wine vinegar
Salt
Freshly ground pepper

Trim the mustard green stalks so that about 1 inch of the stem is left on. Wash very well to remove all dirt and grit. Discard any yellowing or bruised leaves.

Heat the olive oil and garlic in a 6-quart heavy pot for about 1 minute, or until the garlic starts to sizzle. Add the mustard greens, cover, and simmer for about 20 to 25 minutes or just until the greens turn a dark green, and are tender and wilted.

While the greens are simmering, blend the anchovies, olives, capers and vinegar until pureed. Reserve.

Remove the cover after the greens are cooked, and evaporate the liquid over medium heat for about 2 minutes. Stir in the vinegar mixture and season with salt and pepper.

To serve, give each person a portion of greens along with the liquid that remains in the pot. Serve with pork, roast lamb or beef. You may also serve this dish as an appetizer.

Peas with Lettuce and Cream

Makes 4 servings

The combination of peas, onions and lettuce is typically French. The greens lend a certain sweetness to the vegetable. I have used frozen peas because few people like to shell their own. Do, of course, use fresh if you possibly can, and if you do, use about 1½ cups of shelled peas as the equivalent of one package of frozen.

1 head of Boston lettuce, washed
5 tablespoons butter
1 medium-size onion, thinly sliced
10-ounce package of frozen "petite" peas, thawed
2 tablespoons heavy cream
Salt
Freshly ground pepper

Stack the lettuce leaves, and roll them up tightly so that they look like fat cigars. Cut them into cross pieces, about ¼ inch thick. They should unroll into fine shreds.

Heat the butter in a 9-inch skillet. Add onion, and sauté for about 7 minutes or until the onion is translucent. Add the lettuce shreds and sauté until wilted. Add the peas and cream and reduce over medium heat, for about 3 minutes, or until the peas are warmed through. Season to taste with salt and pepper.

Potato Sauté

Makes 4 servings

You can make this recipe in advance and reheat it just before serving. As you reheat the potatoes, the skins will tend to stick to the pan. In fact, this helps form delightful crunchy bits, nestled in the soft potatoes.

1½ pounds boiling potatoes, washed and unpeeled
6 tablespoons olive oil
6 tablespoons scallions, finely sliced
Salt
Freshly ground pepper

Dice the potatoes into approximately ½-inch squares.

Heat the olive oil in a 9-inch skillet. When it is hot, add the potatoes. Take care as you do this, because the potatoes will spatter as they touch the hot oil. Cover the skillet, lower the heat and cook for 20 minutes, over fairly low heat. Shake the pan occasionally or stir the potatoes around with a spatula to prevent them from sticking too much.

Remove the cover and raise the heat; sauté for another 5 minutes or until they begin to get crunchy. Add the scallions, salt and pepper and sauté for another minute or so.

Sautéed Escarole with Pancetta

Too often thought of as just a salad ingredient, escarole is also a wonderful cooked vegetable. Its slightly bitter flavor is accented here by a good dose of garlic. Pancetta is an unsmoked bacon. If you can't find it, use nitrite-free bacon, which you should first parboil for a couple of minutes to rid it of its smoky taste.

1½ pounds escarole
3 tablespoon butter
3 ounces pancetta, finely chopped
1½ teaspoons garlic, minced
Salt
Freshly ground pepper

Wash the escarole under cold water, leaf by leaf, to rid it of all grit. Discard any bruised or blemished leaves. Tear the leaves into 2-inch pieces.

Bring 4 quarts of water to a rolling boil in a large saucepan. In 2 or 3 batches, parboil escarole for 1 minute and immediately refresh it under cold water to stop the cooking process. When all the escarole is done and cool enough to handle, squeeze out the excess moisture with your hands and set aside.

Place the butter and pancetta in a 9-inch skillet. Sauté until the pancetta is crisp. Turn the burner off. Allow to cool for 45 seconds, and then add the garlic. Sauté for about 30 seconds. Add the escarole, ½ teaspoon salt and ¼ teaspoon pepper. Sauté for about 3 to 4 minutes, or until the escarole is tender and hot.

Spinach, Currants and Walnut Sauté

Makes 4 servings

The ground walnuts soak up the butter and Madeira and make these cling to each spinach leaf. I prefer to use currants because they are smaller than raisins and make more delicate elements in each mouthful.

¼ cup currants, or raisins
4 tablespoons Madeira
1 pound fresh spinach
4 tablespoons butter
½ cup walnuts, ground
Salt
Freshly ground pepper

Soak the currants in the Madeira.

Carefully wash the spinach, making sure to remove all traces of sand and dirt. Remove the stems.*

Heat the butter in a large skillet. When it is hot, add the currants with Madeira and sauté for about 30 seconds. Add the spinach leaves in small batches. With tongs, swish the spinach around in the butter and Madeira until it is just barely wilted. Add the walnuts, ½ teaspoon salt and ¼ teaspoon pepper. Serve immediately, along with the pan juices.

Stir-Fried Watercress with Carrots

Makes 4 servings

When trying to come up with recipes that are interesting and quick to prepare, I always arrive at the same conclusion: If I can't spend time on a recipe, then I have to spend money on the ingredients to get the best. In this case, the expensive walnut oil makes the difference in taste.

2 bunches of watercress (8 ounces)
½ pound carrots, peeled
3 tablespoons walnut oil
Salt, to taste
Freshly ground pepper, to taste

Rinse the watercress in cold water. You do not have to dry it. Remove and discard 2 inches from stems and chop what is left into 2-inch pieces.

Grate the carrots coarsely, on the large holes of a hand-held grater or in a food processor.

Heat the walnut oil in a 10-inch skillet. Stir in the carrots and sauté, over high heat, for about 30 seconds. Add the watercress and stir it around until just wilted. Season with salt and pepper and serve immediately.

Swiss Chard with Pear

Swiss chard is a slightly sweet green and is accented here by the addition of a pear puree. It is a change from spinach and is equally rich in vitamins.

2 pounds fresh Swiss chard
1 medium-size pear, preferably
  Comice
4 tablespoons butter
¼ teaspoon thyme
Salt
Freshly ground pepper

Wash the Swiss chard very well to rid it of all sand and dirt. Separate the white ribs from the green leaves. Cut the white ribs into 2-inch pieces.

Peel and core the pear and puree it until liquefied in a blender or food processor. Set aside.*

Heat 1 tablespoon of the butter in a 9-inch skillet. Add the white ribs, cover, and simmer over low heat for 15 minutes. Stir the chard ribs around every now and then. While the ribs are cooking, tear the green leaves into 2-inch pieces.

After 15 minutes, add the leaves, cover, and simmer for 5 minutes, stirring the chard every now and then.

Remove the cover. Add the pear puree, thyme, ¾ teaspoon salt and ¼ teaspoon pepper with remaining butter. Stir until all the butter is melted. Serve immediately, making sure to spoon the juices over the chard.

Zucchini and Dill

This is a plain recipe which is easy to make and flavorful as well. Steamed zucchini are tossed with a minimum of vinegar and plenty of dill. I prefer the subtle, soft taste of rice vinegar, but you may use one with a more acidic tang.

1½ pounds zucchini, washed and stemmed
1 tablespoon rice vinegar
2 tablespoons fresh dill, finely chopped
Salt
Freshly ground pepper

Julienne the zucchini in approximately 2-by-¼-inch strips. Bring 1 inch of water to a boil in a 4-quart saucepan. Add a vegetable steamer. Place the zucchini in the steamer. Cover, and steam, over medium heat, for about 3 minutes, or until the zucchini is just cooked and still bright green. Drain the zucchini and pat dry with towels. Arrange the pieces in a bowl with vinegar and dill. Toss with salt and pepper. Serve immediately as they cool quickly.

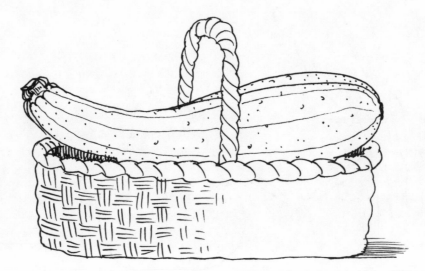

DESSERTS

Pear Brown Betty

Makes 6 servings

Use ripe pears for this dessert so that the flavor of the fruit comes through. You could use unripe pears, but the dessert would end up tasting like apple, not pear, brown betty. You can make cookie crumbs by crushing tea biscuits, with a rolling pin, between sheets of wax paper.

2 cups (8 ounces) cookie crumbs
½ cup brown sugar
½ teaspoon ground nutmeg
2 pounds ripe Comice pears, peeled, cored and sliced thinly
2 tablespoons Cognac or brandy
6 tablespoons butter, cut into ½-inch dice
½ cup sour cream

Preheat oven to 375 degrees.

Butter an 8-by-8-inch baking pan and set aside.

Combine the cookie crumbs with the brown sugar and nutmeg.

Scatter about one-third of the crumb mixture on bottom of baking pan. Place half the pears on top of that; sprinkle half the Cognac on pears, and dot with half the butter. Repeat with half the remaining crumbs and all the remaining ingredients, in above order. Cover with the remaining crumbs.*

Bake for 25 to 30 minutes, or until the pears are tender.

Serve with a spoonful of sour cream for each person.

Coffee Chocolate Chip Cookies

Makes 20 2-inch cookies

This is a special version of a chocolate chip cookie. Instead of using packaged chips, try using bits of chocolate which you cut up yourself. If you do, you will be making cookies the way the original Toll House cookies were done. The addition of oil tenderizes the dough. If you cannot find walnut oil, use peanut oil. It is essential that you choose an excellent brand of semi-sweet chocolate, such as an imported Swiss brand.

6 ounces semi-sweet chocolate, at room temperature
10 tablespoons butter, at room temperature, plus 1 for greasing cookie sheets
1 cup flour, plus 1 tablespoon for preparing cookie sheets
6 tablespoons brown sugar
10 tablespoons granulated sugar
¼ teaspoon salt
1 whole egg
1½ tablespoons instant coffee, preferably espresso
2 tablespoons walnut oil
½ cup walnuts, chopped

Preheat oven to 375 degrees.

Cut the chocolate, with a sharp knife, into pieces approximately ½ inch in size.

With 1 tablespoon of butter, lightly grease 2 cookie sheets. Lightly flour them with 1 tablespoon of flour and shake off the excess.

Cream the butter together with sugars and salt until light and creamy looking. Beat in the egg, coffee and walnut oil.

Stir in the flour and beat until just combined. Add the cut-up chocolate and walnuts.* Refrigerate for 15 minutes.

Spoon about 2 tablespoons of batter, per cookie, onto the prepared cookie sheets. You should get about 10 cookies per sheet. Bake for 10 to 12 minutes. Cool on a cookie rack.

Hot Apricots in Butter Sauce

Makes 4-6 servings

The servings may appear stingy, but the recipe is so fattening and filling that spare portions seem generous.

½ cup heavy cream, chilled
6 ounces, or 1 cup, packed, dried apricots
½ cup water
¼ cup sugar plus 2 teaspoons
¼ cup sliced almonds
1 tablespoon Armagnac or other brandy
¼ teaspoon almond extract
2 tablespoons butter

Whip the heavy cream until stiff in a chilled bowl, with chilled beaters. Reserve in a bowl, covered, in the refrigerator. Place the apricots in a 2-quart saucepan. Cover with ½ cup water; bring the water to a boil and simmer over very low heat for 5 minutes, covered. After 5 minutes, add ¼ cup sugar and continue to simmer, covered, for 3 minutes more. Then remove the cover and evaporate the water. The apricots should then be shiny and glistening in the sugar syrup.

Meanwhile, toss the sliced almonds over medium heat, in

a small skillet without any fat. Stir them continually or they will burn. When they begin to brown, add the remaining 2 teaspoons sugar and continue to stir them over medium heat. The sugar will begin to melt and adhere to the almonds. The sugar never quite caramelizes, but some almonds will take on a golden hue and a sticky quality. Remove from the heat and reserve for garnish.

Add the Armagnac and almond extract to apricots.* Return them to the heat and whisk in the butter. Remove from heat.

To serve, spoon some cold whipped cream in the bottom of the dessert bowls and spoon hot buttered apricots over the cream; sprinkle the sugared almonds on top.

Coffee Sabayon

Makes 4 servings

This is the perfect dessert to make when you don't have many ingredients on hand. You may use all Cognac or brandy instead of half and half Tia Maria. Although I prefer the light, airy, hot texture, you may freeze this, once it is finished, and serve it the next day.

6 egg yolks
1½ tablespoons instant espresso coffee
¼ cup Cognac
¼ cup Tia Maria
¾ cup confectioners' sugar

With an electric hand-held beater, whisk all the ingredients together, using 1 tablespoon of instant coffee only (reserve the rest for garnish). Beat until frothy.

Place this in the top part of a double boiler. Then bring water to a boil in the bottom part of the boiler.

Place the pan containing the mixture on top of the hot water and beat for several minutes until the mixture is very frothy, thick and light. Pour into large goblets and eat immediately before it deflates. Dust the tops lightly with instant coffee before serving.

Floating Islands with Lemon Crème Anglaise

Makes 4 servings

There are a couple of things to beware of before starting to make this recipe. When cooking the crème Anglaise, do not stop whisking or the eggs will scramble. Do not poach the meringues at too high a heat or they will have an unpleasant taste and tough texture. If you avoid these pitfalls, you will have a winning dessert to add to your repertoire.

½ cup milk
¼ cup heavy cream
4 egg yolks
¼ cup lemon juice
½ teaspoon lemon rind, grated
⅓ cup sugar plus 6 tablespoons
3 egg whites
Salt

Bring the milk and cream just to a boil, and instantly remove from heat.

Whisk the yolks, lemon juice, rind and ⅓ cup of sugar for about 2 minutes, or until the mixture looks sticky and pale yellow. Whisk the hot milk and cream into the egg yolks and lemon. Return this mixture to a saucepan and stir constantly, with a wooden spoon, over low heat until the crème Anglaise thickens slightly. When it is about to thicken, you will see lots of steam rising from the saucepan. To be positive, use a candy thermometer. Remove the mixture from heat the minute it thickens, or when the candy thermometer registers 175 degrees. Continue to stir to cool the mixture. Refrigerate.*

Line a baking pan with wax paper.

Beat the egg whites with a pinch of salt until semi-stiff. Add 6 tablespoons of sugar, very gradually, and beat until whites look glossy and very white.

Bring about 2 inches of water just to a simmer in a shallow saucepan. Spoon 3-inch rounds of egg-white meringues into the simmering water and repeat until the saucepan is full but not crowded. Simmer the meringues about 2 minutes per side. With a slotted spoon, remove the "islands" to the prepared baking pan.

Leave them at room temperature until you are ready to serve them. To serve, spoon some lemon crème Anglaise in the bottom of the serving bowl and float room-temperature "islands" on top.

Prune Mousse with Chocolate Sauce

Makes 6 servings

The taste of prunes, Armagnac and chocolate is really special. I hope that this recipe will tempt even the most ardent prune-haters to try it and will alter their opinion of this misunderstood fruit.

1½ cups pitted prunes
1 tablespoon powdered,
   unsweetened cocoa
¼ cup Armagnac
1 cup heavy cream
3 egg whites
¼ cup sugar
1 tablespoon confectioners' sugar

Sauce:
⅔ cup semi-sweet chocolate bits
¼ cup Armagnac

Puree the prunes, cocoa, Armagnac, and ¼ cup of heavy cream in a food mill, or a food processor. Puree until smooth.

Beat the egg whites with a pinch of salt and whip until semi-stiff. Gradually, a tablespoon at a time, add the sugar and beat until the egg whites are stiff and glossy. Fold this into the prune puree and refrigerate.

Whip the remaining heavy cream in a cold bowl, with chilled beaters until semi-stiff. Add confectioners' sugar and beat until stiff. Fold this into the prune mousse and refrigerate.*

Melt the chocolate with ¼ cup water and Armagnac in a small saucepan. Stir as the chocolate melts. The minute the chocolate has melted, remove it from the heat.

To serve, spoon a portion of prune mousse on each plate and spoon chocolate sauce over that. There will be a small portion with only a bit of sauce because this is so rich.

NOTE: You may substitute brandy for the Armagnac.

Pumpkin Mousse

Makes 6-8 servings

Traditional recipes for pumpkin pies and desserts are too spicy for my taste and obliterate what there is of any pumpkin taste. This mousse, therefore, is relatively unspicy. The chopped apricots and pecans make a pleasant textural contrast to the smooth mousse, and add a tangy, unexpected flavor.

¾ cup dried apricots
3 tablespoons rum
1-pound can unsweetened pumpkin
   pie filling
4 tablespoons butter, melted
½ cup brown sugar
¼ teaspoon each of ground allspice,
   cinnamon, and nutmeg
½ cup pecans, chopped
¾ cup heavy cream

Combine the dried apricots with the rum in a small pot with a tight-fitting lid. Bring this to a boil, and simmer over low heat for 1 minute. Cover, and let the apricots cool in the covered pot.

Place the pumpkin in a mixing bowl; whisk in the melted butter, sugar and spices; stir in the chopped nuts. When the apricots are cool, cut them into ½-inch pieces and stir them—and any remaining liquid in the pot—into the mousse. Chill.

While the mousse is chilling, whip the heavy cream until it is very stiff. Fold most of it into the mousse, reserving some for decoration. Chill until ready to eat.*

Just before serving, spoon the mousse into large wine goblets and pipe some whipped cream in the center of each mousse, with a pastry bag.

Oranges in Grand Marnier

This is a classic French recipe, which also goes by the name of Oranges Orientale. It is refreshing and light—perfect as an ending to a hearty winter repast or to a cool summer supper. Try to search for a fresh vanilla bean; it makes all the difference in the world.

1 or 2 navel or other eating oranges, per person, depending on size

2 to 3 tablespoons superfine sugar, or to taste

1 tablespoon Grand Marnier, or to taste

2-inch piece of fresh vanilla bean

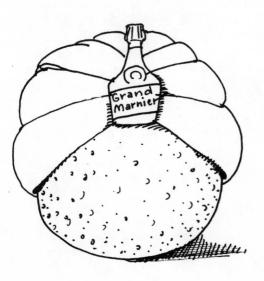

Peel the oranges by holding them over a bowl to catch all the juices. Pare them to remove the rind and white pith. Cut each orange in half down the vertical line. You will then see a thick white core inside. Cut that out as completely as you can. Then lay the orange half on a cutting board with the flat side down; cut perpendicular to the orange segments, thus forming crescents about ¼ inch thick. Transfer these to a bowl with as much of the juice as possible. Repeat with all the oranges. Taste the juice. If it is not very sweet, then add all the sugar or more to taste. Do the same with the Grand Marnier.

Split the vanilla bean in half, lengthwise. You will see the insides, glistening with the shiny seeds. Scrape these black seeds into the oranges, and mix them in. Stick the vanilla pod in the oranges as well.

Cover with plastic wrap and marinate as long as possible.* (You could, of course, eat them right away.)

Just before serving, remove the vanilla pod.

To serve, spoon some of the oranges along with the juice into glass bowls or large wine goblets.

Chocolate Soufflés with Raspberry Cream

Makes 4 servings

The taste is so intense that these soufflés taste like hot pôts de crème. *If you don't like the flavor of raspberries with chocolate, substitute some liqueur in the accompanying whipped cream.*

**2 teaspoons butter for greasing
   ramekins**
1 tablespoon sugar
⅓ cup heavy cream
1 tablespoon confectioners' sugar
**10-ounce package frozen raspberries
   in syrup, thawed**
2 ounces semi-sweet chocolate
1 ounce unsweetened chocolate
¼ cup milk
2 egg yolks
3 egg whites
1½ tablespoons sugar

Preheat oven to 400 degrees.

Butter 4 ½-cup ramekins and lightly dust the insides with sugar. Set aside.

Whip the cream in a chilled bowl, with chilled beaters. When semi-stiff add the confectioners' sugar and beat until stiff. Refrigerate.

Drain the raspberries and puree them until smooth. Then force them through a small sieve in order to remove the seeds. Fold the raspberry puree into the whipped cream and set aside, covered, in a bowl in the refrigerator.*

Place the chocolates with the milk in a small saucepan. Melt over low heat, stirring constantly. The minute all the chocolate has melted, remove from the heat and transfer the chocolate to a small bowl. Whisk the egg yolks into the chocolate, one at a time. Beat the egg whites with a pinch of salt until they are at the soft peak stage. Then add the sugar and beat until very stiff, but not dry. Fold a quarter of the whites into the chocolate mixture to lighten it and then fold the lightened chocolate mixture back into the egg whites.

Bake for 10 to 12 minutes; the soufflés should remain moist in the center.

To serve, bring the soufflés to the table. Break each one open with a spoon and add raspberry cream in the center of each soufflé.

Hazelnut Chocolate Pôts de Crème

Makes 6 servings

1 cup whole hazelnuts
3 egg yolks
6 ounces semi-sweet chocolate
2 tablespoons butter, at room
   temperature
2 egg whites
½ cup superfine sugar
½ cup chilled whipped cream

You will need a blender or food processor for this recipe. After you roast the nuts, you must pulverize them in such a way as to release the nut oils, which in turn release all the flavor.

Preheat oven to 400 degrees.

Put the hazelnuts in a baking pan and roast them for 15 to 20 minutes, or until they emit a lovely toasted aroma. Remove from oven and let cool for 5 minutes. Place them in towels and rub them hard. The toasted skins should flake off easily; do not worry about those that do not.

Process the hazelnuts in a blender or food processor for about a minute, or until they become oily. Add the yolks to the processor and blend until the yolks and nuts are combined.

Melt the chocolate in a double boiler until chocolate is soft. Remove from the heat and stir in the butter. The chocolate will lose its glossy quality at this point and stiffen somewhat. Add the nuts and yolks to the chocolate.

Whip the egg whites with a pinch of salt until semi-stiff. Add the sugar, tablespoon by tablespoon, until the egg whites are very stiff and shiny. Fold this into chocolate mixture until no more white shows; spoon this mixture into ½-cup ramekins.*

Just before serving, pipe a whipped cream rosette in the center of each mousse.